"Curriculum scholars and practitioners disposed to Modernist representational discourses in which 'thought precedes language' will find *Writing Research/Researching Writing: Through a Poet's I* excitingly provocative. Readers are beckoned to a re-positioned linguistic site of inter-textuality wherein language doubly informs and performs to produce effects. So located, Gary William Rasberry both explores *and* lives in the textured signifying site of writing/reading research such that 'researching pedagogy' is not merely researching *about* pedagogy, but also allows in and through the signifying practice of writing/reading constituting and reconstituting pedagogy. Moreover, in an uncanny way, Rasberry allows texts to speak such that readers may find themselves participating in their own textual transformation."

— Ted T. Aoki, Professor Emeritus, University of Alberta

"'Poetry outside of writing poems, then, has something to say about lines *and* lives: it has something to say about research.' So writes Gary William Rasberry in a book that brings together the somethings of living and teaching. Throughout this passionate reimagining of scholarly experience, Rasberry invites us in with his words: tangle, tendril, desire, obsession, snippet, counterclockwise. Words for this poet-teacher are not pointers to the outside of lived experience; they offer forms of knowing, moment by moment, particularity by particularity. Drawing on curriculum theory, literary writing, and his own poetry, Rasberry offers a dwelling place for those of us seeking ways to live our lives in the classroom and the library with deeper appreciation for the metaphors that surround us every day."

— Mary Aswell Doll, Author of
Like Letters in Running Water: A Mythopoetics of Curriculum

Writing Research/
Researching Writing

Studies in the
Postmodern Theory of Education

Joe L. Kincheloe and Shirley R. Steinberg
General Editors

Vol. 140

PETER LANG
New York • Washington, D.C./Baltimore • Boston • Bern
Frankfurt am Main • Berlin • Brussels • Vienna • Oxford

Gary William Rasberry

Writing Research/ Researching Writing

Through a Poet's I

PE
1404
.R36
2001
West

PETER LANG
New York • Washington, D.C./Baltimore • Boston • Bern
Frankfurt am Main • Berlin • Brussels • Vienna • Oxford

Library of Congress Cataloging-in-Publication Data
Rasberry, Gary William.
Writing research/researching writing:
through a poet's I / Gary William Rasberry.
p. cm. — (Counterpoints; vol. 140)
Includes bibliographical references (p.) and index.
1. English language—Rhetoric—Study and teaching—Research.
2. Poetry—Authorship—Study and teaching—Research.
3. Creative writing—Study and teaching—Research. I. Title.
II. Counterpoints (New York, N.Y.); vol. 140.
PE1404 .R36   808'.042071—dc21   00-062978
ISBN 0-8204-4923-7
ISSN 1058-1634

Die Deutsche Bibliothek-CIP-Einheitsaufnahme
Rasberry, Gary William:
Writing research/researching writing:
through a poet's I / Gary William Rasberry.
–New York; Washington, D.C./Baltimore; Boston; Bern;
Frankfurt am Main; Berlin; Brussels; Vienna; Oxford: Lang.
(Counterpoints; Vol. 140)
ISBN 0-8204-4923-7

The paper in this book meets the guidelines for permanence and durability
of the Committee on Production Guidelines for Book Longevity
of the Council of Library Resources.

Printed in the United States of America

ACKNOWLEDGMENTS

I. Your Careful Listening

I have so much to thank you for,
the sky falling out in colors
just this way.

The blue is in the exchange
knowing I need you
to complete the seeing.

Who would I be without you
to read the thin line of clouds
that gather sometimes

on certain afternoons as if
in anticipation of a prairie
sunset. And

who would know god went by
if it weren't for your careful listening.

And the quiet rain that falls afterward
on small green coastal towns making gray
so worthy of praise?

The page must be turned in faith
with the understanding that words
will grace the other side.

The wind providing the illusion
of a hawk in flight
means we are being written.

The ferry makes the islands possible and
the ocean is everything else left over
in the language of our living.

II. A Series of Acknowledgings

mindful of breath, of thoughts
small in their singing, the light falling
out as citations left   unformatted.

the page winding up empty or crowded
over with weeds that spell beauty   backwards.
Ending by beginning by
ending: thankful

for every thing. for *a bowl of yellow flowers*. for the *freezing
music*. for *wildmind*. *for writing
down the bones*: karen connelly. al purdy. natalie goldberg.

to the teacher candidates in ened 426:   language across the
curriculum, section *989*, for im-personating themselves, gracious,
even in their pseudonyms.

to gaalen erickson. tony clarke. dennis sumara. for their careful
listening.

to lorri neilsen. rita irwin. george mcwhirter. graeme chalmers.
for burning close to the candle.

to david jardine. maria klawe. john willinsky. margery fee. ted
aoki. allan mackinnon. mary aswell doll. and deborah britzman
(for the curious time of pedagogy).
to joe l. kincheloe and shirley r. steinberg

for family: jean peter coosje linda tom sydney matthew and
courtney. ziggy valda ivar sylvie brencis kora and marcis.
and in memory: leonard charles rasberry.
for extended family: janet angus bridget and kelsey.

for fecundity and fixity and flux and a life that includes writing. a
broad stone wall flicking alive small green flames of lizards. live
music. stubborn particulars. neil & bruce. my complete line of
espresso-makers, brass-bellied stovetoppers, which remain

unfailing in their impeccable sense of timing. the marginalia that overwhelm with textual underpinnings. the crazy need to measure mystery. for certainty questioned.

poetryfictionpoetryfictionpoetryfictionpoetryfictionpoetryfictionp oetryfictionpoetryfictionpoetry

to carl leggo: for the poet's gift of un/naming.

to steve elliott: for gracing the front   cover.

for the generous support of the social sciences and humanities research council of canada, for doctoral and postdoctoral fellowships.

for gathered poetry found lying
in the margins, in/visible only to itself.

and the metaphysical candle that heats up the winding out, burning away to beat the night into a band of light.

and always, for fear and for forgetting to
save as...

and closer to home: the oldstone schoolhouse, all woodstove and windows. and treasures, too.
paws for reflection: magpie. buzz. toobie. forbes. the reign of cats and dogs.

for hayden: original blessing. for zinta: original blessing, too/two.

and first and finally: to rena.
to whom I am so grateful. always. and ever.
    rena brigit upitis: who invents the world each day. for our living together in a place where words seem to trip over themselves in their effort to tell the whole   story.

* * *

The author would like to acknowledge the following for permission to reprint excerpts and poems from the works listed below:

Leggo, C., A poet's pensées: Writing and schooling. _English Quarterly_, 23(3–4): 4–10. Montreal, QC: Canadian Council of Teachers of English and Language Arts, McGill University Printing Service, copyright, 1992. Reprinted by permission of the publisher. All rights reserved.

Rasberry, G. W., Trust me I'm a doctor: Healing the wounded writer? _English Quarterly_, 26(2): 17–20. Montreal, QC: Canadian Council of Teachers of English and Language Arts, McGill University Printing Service, copyright, 1994. Reprinted by permission of the publisher. All rights reserved.

Rasberry, G. W., Finding form. _Journal of Curriculum Theorizing_, 13(4): 46–49. Toronto, ON: Corporation of Curriculum Research, inside/out, copyright, 1997. Reprinted by permission of the publisher. All rights reserved.

* * *

Excerpts from students' writing are reprinted with permission. Pseudonyms are used throughout.

Cover design by Stephen Elliott, Kingston, ON. Adaptation of an original work by Stephen Elliott, titled "Apples and Pips".

* * *

CONTENTS

Foreword   xi
Lorri Neilsen

An Opening   xiii

Preface: The Educational Research Fanzine: xv
A Record of Obsession

1   Through a Poet's I   1

2   A Bowl of Yellow Flowers Stains the Canvas   13

3   A Life That Includes Writing   55

4   Through the Tangle   99

5   The Curious Time of Researching Pedagogy   129

6   Teachers Writing Lives   165

Postscript   197

References   199

FOREWORD

Where do we look to feed the spirit of teaching and learning? As educators, we tend to gather supplies, store them in a space to draw upon some day. But as of late, the education pantry has become crowded, oppressive. The shelves are bent with the bulk of recipe books, some as sallow and weathered as their owners. The floor is covered in layers of tile, each laid in its own time with certainty and a whopping amount of glue. We cannot see the ceiling. We cannot stretch our arms. We cannot find a window; cupboards crammed with quick mix and easy packaging occlude our view. Overprocessed words—ordered, wrapped, and stocked—are stuffed inside this space. We cannot move.

And we know, in the words of William Carlos Williams, that we can die miserably for lack of what is found there.

Remember when a word was a breath, a song, a drink of cool water, a glint of silver in a rock, a dance? Remember when learning and living in and around words were the delicious taste that brought us eagerly to the pantry, the melody that lifted our feet, the play that brought us laughter, tears, hope?

Remember when the times of wordplay were rough, where, as Denise Levertov reminds us, we scraped our knees on rosy stone, and then suddenly, wings brushed past, and the poem ascended?

Gary William Rasberry does; he dares to imagine a space where we do not hoard supplies and stock shelves, but where there is light and the promise of creation; where the garden we see from the window offers all we need to nourish us. Throw out the packages, clear a space for many people to turn over words, cut and mix them, infuse them with their particular seasoning, share them, draw their strength for learning and living. Tear down the shelves and make room for an airy bright space that is open to the sun. Imagine. We have all we need here.

It's a space we must create for the spirit of learning and teaching writing to survive, but we have not made it. *Writing Research/Researching Writing: Through a Poet's I* offers wisdom and sparkling insights that can guide us. We write our teaching. We write our learning. They write us. And in working with words—Rasberry calls it "wording"—we write ourselves. In researching words we write research. This is an organic, fluid, process. It is never over. Writing our lives as teachers and writers is not a process we can escape with predictions. We need an openness, time, faith.

If, as Gaston Bachelard has written, the life lived in poetry is "the phenomenology of the soul," this work gives us cause for hope. The twentieth century has been a bumpy ride; we have lurched simplistically, almost mechanically, through the tensions of individual/social, process/product, formal/informal, reader/text, poetic/transactional. Our guides have been Vygotsky and Jakobson, Britton, Kelly, Rosenblatt, Emig, among others. Whether it is among school children or preservice teachers, we have looked at writing pedagogy variously as something we must construct and dissemble, seek and harness, learn and then teach, know and then tell. To understand where Rasberry is taking us here is to understand the body swaying to music that Yeats writes of; to live inside words, where the soul keeps watch and we learn that we cannot, nor do we want to, tell the dancer from the dance.

What you are about to read "complexifies" what needs to be made complex, and yet the message remains simple. Rasberry fuses teaching/writing/lives in ways that more accurately tell what we know and don't know, do and do not do. The writing becomes in itself the ontological issues he raises. The words about words here are ambitious, sparkling, impassioned, witty, innovative, and yes, soulful.

This work begins a needed conversation, gives us pause about our preoccupation with pausing, with evaluating, defining, naming, and fixing tiles to the floor. The stunning effect of this brilliant transgression of what we've come to expect of academic writing is stimulating and educative. Get ready; this is a semiotic feast. But come with hands full; we will not only share it, but create it as well.

The dazzling effect of this work explodes in moments of significance and joy, just as teaching and writing will do when we give them air and room. This work dares us to imagine. It draws us out of a pantry we no longer need and brings us into the sun.

Lorri Neilsen
Mount Saint Vincent University
Halifax, Nova Scotia

Imagining the Curious Time of Researching Pedagogy[1]

Imagine: a trail made of moments
rather than minutes, wild bits
according to a schedule.

Pauses.

Each one bell-shaped,
into which you step
as an applicant
for the position of tongue.

Or: each pause is designed as
the unbuilt dwelling of that moment—a cabin,
a stanza, a gazebo, a frame—a room
which the trail accepts as a fiction or a   wish.

This is the point of [Time
in Teacher Education], the erotic hinge of translation.
When ownership is set aside,
appropriation can turn inside
out,   an opening,   a way of
going up to something with a gift   from home...

...[textual play]...along this trail, is a gift
to the other from the dwelling
you will never build there.

How?

A slight deformation of human categories,
an extra metaphorical stretch and silliness
of language as it moves toward the other,

---

[1] I begin imagining the curious time of researching pedagogy through a poetic absconding of Canadian poet Don McKay's words. The particular passage of his prose I have poeticized comes from an essay entitled "Binder twine: thoughts on ravens, home and nature poetry," in which he contemplates/questions "poetry and knowing". (Lilburn 1995)

dreaming its body. There is danger

in this gift, because language,
in this poetic mode, compromises
its nature, dismantl[es]   itself...

[Researchers]/Poets
are supremely interested
in what language can't do;
in order to gesture   outside, they use language
in a way that flirts
with its destruction...

The Educational Research Fanzine: A Record of Obsession

Never does one open the discussion by coming right to the heart of the matter. For the heart of the matter is always somewhere else than where it is supposed to be.

—Trinh T. Minh-ha, *Woman, Native, Other*, 1989.

Throughout the long and sometimes arduous but always privileged period in which this book has taken shape, I have been tempted, again and again, to re-present the piece of work that follows as it has presented itself to me—as a dis/continuous series; an oddly portioned and multifarious collection of words that seem to beg for something other than chapters as places, placeholders, that might provide them with some kind of home, some kind of form in which to find themselves.

Perhaps I have been reading too much Roland Barthes, whose words, often irreverent in their scholarly musings, offer such pearly wisdoms as: "Thus every writer's motto reads: *mad I cannot be, sane I do not deign to be, neurotic I am*" (1975, 6). Or perhaps some of my not-so-clandestine poetic and fictional explorations, unconventional needles that cannot be separated out from the haystack of my ongoing scholarly harvests, have convinced me, truly, that all of my/our writings are simply sidebars and/or marginalia in a world where writing wishes it were otherwise.

Throughout the writing of this book, the nighttable has held steady under the press of books: the unbearable lightness of Kundera, the sometimes acerbic Rushdie; the poetry-filled prose of Anne Michaels; the Canadian fiction hall-of-famers: Munro, Ondaatje, Gallant, Shields. Poetry and more poetry: Kate Braid, Joy Kogawa, Seamus Heaney, Bronwen Wallace, Karen Connelly, Bill Bissett, Patrick Lane. Collections of essays by Wendell Berry, Oliver Sacks, Annie Dillard, Linda Hutcheon, Daphne Marlatt, Rafael Campo, Jeanette Winterson. All these, along with tricksters like John Barth rewriting many of my (conventional) notions of writing, or Italo Calvino serving up several opening chapters, promising always a beginning, delivering instead a playful circling; offering mock consolation at every turn: "And you realize ...alert reader that you are...that, to tell the truth, everything was slipping through your fingers" (Calvino 1981, 37).

So why do I bother offering you my nightstand of book titles amid what will surely include an already overcrowded desktop's worth of educational hardcovers and scholarly research journals? I mention these writings and their authors as a kind of acknowledgment. An acknowledgment of the vital role they have played in the writing of this book—not as pleasant distractions from the "real business" of scholarly inquiry but as inextricable, invaluable pieces of the complex web of curricular relations required to make an endeavor such as this possible.

While I name such works—of fiction, and poetry, and essays of one form or another—in order to acknowledge the obvious but often unannounced influences they may have had while this research dreamed me, there is more. (Certainly, they have offered everything from comfort to inspiration when I felt that things were truly slipping through my fingers.) These literary works also announce, in what I hope will become evident in the pages that follow, my passion for *a life that includes reading.*[1] And writing. For a life that includes words and wordmaking. And wonder. And, finally, for a life that seeks to engage with others whose lives also include reading and writing, learning and teaching. Emphatically (and ungrammatically) speaking, I cannot *not* mention these works, just as I do not wish to make them separate from the curricular artists who have helped shape the pedagogical and aesthetic sensibilities of this life project without end:

Bitter milk   Pedagon   Practice Makes Practice   Teaching to Transgress
Madeleine Grumet   David Smith   Deborah Britzman   bell hooks

---

[1] "A Life That Includes Reading," is the title of the opening chapter of Dennis Sumara's (1996a) *Private Readings in Public: Schooling the Literary Imagination.* I have borrowed the expression and added a variation by exchanging "reading" with "writing." Chapter 2, "A Life That Includes Writing," explores what the interplay of these two words—reading and writing—might mean to our lives lived in and out of classrooms.

Private Readings in Public   Releasing the Imagination   Speaking With a
Dennis Sumara   Maxine Greene   David Jardine   Patti Lather
Boneless Tongue   Getting Smart   Teaching Mathematics: Toward A Sound
Brent Davis   Bill Pinar   Adrienne Rich   William Gass   Mary Doll
Alternative   Understanding Curriculum   What Is Found There   The World
John Caputo   Trinh T. Minh-ha   James Hillman   Jane Gallop
Within the Word To the Lighthouse and Back Radical Hermeneutics Woman,
Hélène Cixous   Ted Aoki   Jacques Daignault   Laurel Richardson
Native, Other   Puer Papers   Pedagogy: The Question of Impersonation

A partial list to be sure, but certainly enough to evoke poetry. For poetry, in my view, often *is* a list, and, in turn, I list these writers and their various writings just as I might attend to a favorite poem, or invent an incantation that helps to ritualize my curricular practice—a deliberate and ceremonious weaving of particular objects, artifacts, and events. All of this, and yet there is something else. Something more.

The poet Adrienne Rich says, "You must write, and read, as if your life depended on it. That is not generally taught in school" (1993, 32). She continues,

> To read as if your life depended on it would mean to let into your reading your beliefs, the swirl of your dreamlife, the physical sensations of your ordinary carnal life; and, simultaneously, to allow what you're reading to pierce the routines, safe and impermeable, in which ordinary carnal life is tracked, charted, channeled. (32)

To write and read as if your life depended on it. It's certainly difficult to deny the gravity of Rich's passionate words: *This is not generally taught in school.*[2] And yet, this book, this particular and purposeful turning of energy and attention toward the shared experience of reading and writing and learning and teaching, seeks to imagine education—in the words of Maxine Greene—*as if it could be otherwise.* In her book *Releasing the Imagination,* Greene states that she wants to "help us think in ways that move beyond schooling to the larger domains of education, where there are and must be all kinds of openings to possibility" (1995, 5).

Openings to possibility. This is why I choose to begin this particular body of work with a preface that is in some ways an

---

[2] Repeated instances of previously quoted text are sometimes italicized without page references.

invocation—a calling upon—that seeks openings to possibility, as well as a certain kind of guidance and support from the Muse(s). This is why I begin by placing the work of Maxine Greene and Adrienne Rich alongside Barbara Gowdy and Russell Banks. Teachers, poets, writers: releasing the imagination. Reclaiming the imagination. Inviting us, demanding, even, that we allow what we are reading to, in Rich's words, *pierce the routines* of the ordinary. All of these writers, educators, poets, "each...teaching me to read the other" (Felman 1987, 6).

It is not surprising that a life that includes reading and writing (and teaching) would also include a certain amount of obsession: the capacity to be swallowed up, consumed by words, worlds: wor(l)ds. Lost and found. Lost and found. Lost. In turn, the capacity to learn to live well with both the intense light of obsession as well as the long shadow that often accompanies its presence are important parts of the living. James Hillman says that for every bit of light we grasp—"that bright circle of awareness"—we also darken the remainder of the room (1979, 12). Yet, if we are moved by Rich's words, if we recognize ourselves in her words, knowing *the swirl of our dreamlife*, we might also find strange comfort in obsession, recognize it as one of the many faces of living a life that includes learning and teaching. Reading. Writing. In this way, obsession becomes an acknowledged element, one of the conditions that make certain kinds of teaching and learning, reading and writing possible.

Informed by the busy stirrings of popular culture, my work, in many senses, feels like the production of a *fanzine*: "a record of obsession," as it has been described both by the media and by fanzine-keepers. Originating in the cinematic world, fanzines—put together by obsessive fans, most often as basement operations—can take the form of photocopied sheets unceremoniously hand stapled together, or they might be professionally printed on glossy stock. Reflecting the idiosyncratic bent of their founders, these "zines" tended, historically, to operate as mail order productions dedicated most often to the heady cult(ure) of B-movies. Though I am reticent to carry the B-movie metaphor over to the work to which I have dedicated myself these past days and months and years, I am not at all reluctant to name this particular (curricular) obsession in order to help find a form for my passion, those things for which I care deeply about.

A record of obsession. This is what I find when I look back over my shoulder toward the future. No real beginning, middle. End. Simply a complex gathering of citations, incantations, and ruminations in endless combinations and permutations. Obsession. This is a word I do not often encounter in the field of education(al research). Most often, obsession is something that might best be sidestepped. For fear. Obsession is desire unhinged, or so we say. Not usually used in curricular terms. Yet, it seems an appropriate word to use in the context of our work as writers and teachers and researchers; it lends itself to our becoming curious.

I choose to make obsession a curricular concern, not so that I might loosen its burden through a kind of therapeutic catharsis, but so that I might more mindfully consider its weight, claim it even as I offer it up for consideration within a broader community of teachers and writers and researchers. In offering up my own particulars, and in turn, some of those whose lives have become connected to mine through our shared experiences—in this case of writing and reading and considering the practice of teaching—I hope to render visible, through attention to form,

> some of the "usually-invisible pedagogical relations that circumscribe our teaching and learning". (Sumara and Davis, 1996, 4)

Perhaps my introductory remarks characterizing the research-as-dilemma, as I fumble for form and bring the works of Italo Calvino to bear on those of bell hooks, *are* merely confessional; the bedside table moved into the study as a rhetorically convenient bit of furniture rearrangement. Even so, it is a necessary fumbling in my efforts to establish a location from which to begin to dwell on a specific set of curriculum practices. "The 'private' reading is illusory," says Sumara, "both reading and writing are communal acts" (1996a, xiii). While my own (private) practice of reading and writing are integral to the work, they are not in themselves sufficient nor generous enough as locations for interpretation; they provide a kind of starting place, however, a way of attempting to make visible the oftentimes hidden conditions required to produce something we might agree to call research—or a novel or a poem or a fanzine. I feel it is important and worthwhile to make more explicit the living and writing that is often required to work in the world as a teacher and a researcher. Otherwise, the nightstand conveniently disappears as the names fall into neatly pressed rows of citations (or are left out altogether); the marginalia are erased by the wax and polish of re-presentation. The press of the last fresh font is left to create the first impression.

The writing of this book—this curriculum form—is a co-laboring and like any curriculum form it "emerges from the middle of the mundane and very specific details of daily life"... the pieces present possibilities, as Sumara and Davis (1996) have described them, "possibilities for educational experiences," as objects intended to function as generous locations for interpretation (2–3). And, in what has surely become a kind of hermeneutic mantra for me, it is never just the "things themselves but rather, in the relational space between and among particular objects, artifacts, and events" (Sumara and Davis 1996, 2) that the curricular acts of reading and writing, living and learning take place.

Under the pull of obsession, I can't seem to stop talking about writing, reading about writing, writing about writing, can't seem to be able to stop talking about a life—about lives—that include the practice of writing. Part of my own experience of living a life that includes the practice of writing—a practice which also includes writing about other writing lives—has led to the strangely troubling, strangely satisfying experience of becoming lost in what I now refer to as "the tangle": A teacher. Teachers. A writing life. Writing lives. Teaching. Learning. Reading. Writing. Researching. It appears impossible not to become caught up in the tangle when considering the question of what the experience of living a life that includes the practice of writing might be, especially when the question is lived through the shared experience of writing. Within the context of teacher education, obsession's spell has also led me to consider, through this tangle, how my wondering (researching) is made different when the writing is "attached" to a living that also includes the practice of becoming a teacher.

From the tangle, I can't seem to stop talking about preservice teachers' writing. About preservice teachers' *writing* lives. And, unless I truly have become unhinged, I believe that many of the teachers, with whom I have had the pleasure and privilege of writing, were willing participants in a shared obsession: writing, writing lives. Writing became a real way of imagining a life that included teaching and learning, a way of following words to find out that words lead to other words, a way for teacher candidates[3] to negotiate their identities as teachers. In other words, writing became a way of wording the world, a world of labyrinthian possibility as well as unexpected ends.

Yet another tendril of obsession in the experience of writing this book has involved being caught between living (a) life and writing about it. Fiction writer Kent Nussey describes this phenomenon as "the thing the writer does to himself by withdrawing from the world to write about it."[4] Nussey continues, "the practice of writing, the extended act of creation, might cost the writer the very things he's trying to capture and illumine in his writing."

Therefore, I need, at the outset, to acknowledge this powerful sense of loss that occurs during a project such as this, a loss that, in Nussey's words, seems to happen "because we have taken our eye off the world to write about it." I am discovering that the willingness to own and embrace obsession can lead to an interesting place pedagogically. Following Nussey from fiction to educational research, part of our acknowledged roles as teachers and researchers must involve cutting ourselves off from pedagogy in order to write about it. We are not, then, simply writing *about* pedagogy. We are *writing* pedagogy. We are not only writing *about* lives, we are *writing* lives. Through teachers' I's. Through researchers' I's; through readerly eyes; through writerly eyes; through poets' I's—*as if our lives depended on it.*

Over an extended period of time, my writing life became filled with snippets of (preservice) teachers' writing lives: bits of poetry, e-mail correspondence, written feedback from class, more bits of

---

[3] I use "preservice teachers" and "teacher candidates" interchangeably.
[4] The passages from Kent Nussey are taken from an address titled "The Book of the Grotesque", given at the Kingston School of Writing, Kingston, Ontario, July 1993. His most recent work of fiction is *The War in Heaven*.

poetry. Not knowing what to do with all the words that began to pile up, I simply gathered them together—all the loose scraps of paper that seemed to beg for some kind of order—and stuffed them unceremoniously into a green plastic box with a hinged lid. I returned to the box on an irregular basis and flipped through the paperworks, shuffled them, looked for clues—looked for some thing for which I had no clue I might be looking.

It was at this point, I think, that the fanzine was born. The cut-and-paste-ability of the scores of words was at once my arch-nemesis and great hope. I tried other strategies. I tried, simply, to be quiet and listen to the writing. I experimented with the art of getting to know art as described by novelist Jeanette Winterson: "Suppose we made a pact with a painting and agreed to sit down and look at it, on our own, with no distractions, for one hour...what would we find?" (1996, 8). Like Winterson, I recognized the roughly formed stages of "Increasing discomfort ...increasing distraction...increasing invention...increasing irritation" (9).

Winterson's discovery, her discomfort *as well as* her love and passion for art led her to title the series of resulting essays, *Art Objects*—such a clever and wonderful way of reconfiguring her relations with the things of the world: "Art Objects. The nouns become an active force, not a collector's item. Art Objects" (Winterson 1996, 19). In a similar way to Winterson's experience of developing relations with paintings, my stumblings with teachers' writing lives—their writing, poetry or otherwise—seemed to "object" to my attempts to be with it, especially to my attempts to sort it or use it for my own purposes. Just in case it is not clear, this "problem"—of learning to live well with the difficulty of teachers' writing lives—was my problem. The writing was, well—itself. As Winterson might have said about my time spent with all of these words, my encounters were not the usual "This [writing] has nothing to say to me," but rather, "I have nothing to say to this [writing]. And I desperately wanted to speak" (4).

My ongoing desire, then, is to continue to find ways to speak and also to be quiet. The book feels to me like a long poem for and about poems. And yet it is not really about poems. I continue to look for ways that we might learn to be with our writings and

researchings. My continuing desire to seek ways (of learning) to be with aspects of reading and writing, and teaching and learning—of the living that goes on in our lives—finds parallels in the ways I continue to learn to read and write poetry, fiction, curriculum. I have wondered and wonder still if it is possible to learn to live with our curricular obsessions as we learn to live
  with poems
dwelling with them at length, hovering
around meaning—not meaning

to pick them apart but rather to admire
their unwillingness to mean

one thing, and to imagine other
possibilities for meaning. Learning always

as Shoshana Felman offers:
  to become attentive to the unreadable, the inaudible, the invisible ...

The idea of an educational fanzine does not appear to object to my contradictory whims and wishes—methodologically, pedagogically or otherwise—in its textual recordings that want to become book. As a record of obsession, it seems to capture the complexity of the "dilemma-lived-as-research" in a way that conveys the earnest desire on the part of one who so desperately wants to speak, to write, to make some kind of sense of teachers' writing lives—of teachers *writing* lives—at the same time as it points to the sheer fallibility of such a venture and the consequent need to embrace a kind of living and writing that self-reflexively points out its own foibles as it goes.

Perhaps, if one were daring enough, the fanzine, itself, would be/come the research: a stapled together, show-and-tell kind of textual record of obsession. Or, perhaps if one were even more daring still, the research might be recognized for what it is: a fanzine.

Finding Form[5]

Of course this is how
it must begin: imagining
the world. Standing
on any green hill
at the mercy of all blue
rivers, (re)inventing the colors
of sky and three perfect ravens.

Waiting for the moon to find a form that signals
the planet's giving way
to an inevitable shade borne out of light.

As a matter of course, the palette gives
and receives in combinations until the body
is no longer a body.

Whisper the incantation as it was given,
as breath. Walk around the canvas three times,
counterclockwise, for luck and
momentum:

Wind the world up until it spins
on spit and sweat and the bloody pitch of a
fallen pine. Aware of nothing
but the first drop of rain
repeating itself—
three times counterclockwise,

Putting the hex on cliché: *out of the blue,*
words fall on open fields, plant themselves and
wait for the world to imagine itself
out of a seed, or run its course like an
avalanche down a garden path
ripping up color
as it goes.

---

[5] Rasberry (1997), *Journal of Curriculum Theorizing, 13*(4), 46–49.

tangled lines and lives

an opening

INTERLUDE

THE UNIVERSITY OF BRITISH COLUMBIA

Centre for the Study of
Curriculum and Instruction
Faculty of Education
Vancouver, B.C.
Canada V6T 1Z4
Tel: (604) 822-6052
Fax: (604) 822-8243

ENED 426: Language Across the Curriculum
A Double-Voiced Consent Poem[6]

Preservice Teacher Consent Form
Tangled Lines and Lives
Part Two
Voices from Teachers Writing Lives

Dear Participant,
Dear Carl,

This letter constitutes Part Two of your written consent to
So far, I feel like a bull in a china shop—just waiting to break
participate in the research project—Language Across the
something. My writing background is very limited—I avoid it
Curriculum: An Investigation of the Writing Practices of Pre-
whenever possible. I like working with numbers. I may not be
Service Teachers—outlined below. This study is part of my
bringing the right attitude in with me...I have never been
doctoral research. Please read the letter carefully before signing
creative and the ideas and writing of others in the class makes

---

[6] I have employed a poetic device, the double-voice, in order to (playfully) juxtapose a version of the consent form that participants signed as part of the ethical review process with feedback received from some of the teacher candidates during the early stages of the course. The comments, taken from "exit slips" written at the end of each class, have been scrambled in a purposeful attempt to con/fuse the lines and lives of the teacher candidates.

and feel free to ask any questions regarding the project and your
me feel a little awkward as I don't feel I can measure up, but I
involvement in it.
will certainly try...

Up to this point in the course, you have agreed to participate in
...I even found myself in the mall last week in a bookstore
the initial phase of the research project involving members of
looking for poetry. While browsing I started looking at journals;
ENED 426: Language Across the Curriculum. As discussed earlier,
I haven't kept a journal in about 11 years. I'm finding a need to
the second phase of the study will involve a smaller number of
express myself...Well I have to admit that before this course
students who have agreed to participate more fully by discussing
started, I was really dreading this class. I'm now looking
their experiences with writing and by sharing samples of their
forward to it. I have never taken a course like this before—one
writing. In addition to regular class writing, this smaller group of
that allows me the freedom to express myself as I am. I have
students will be sharing and discussing their writing through
always enjoyed writing but not for others. I, like many, have
audio-taped interviews, personal journal entries, letters, and
learned the game of essay writing. I have often taken time on
e-mail, as well as creative writing (e.g., poetry). Any time spent
my own to express myself and have then thrown away my
outside class will be voluntary and will not exceed 3 hours/week.
thoughts. I must admit this class scares me a little.

In agreeing to participate in this project it must be stressed that:
...I've been losing sleep, getting tangled in words and writing
1.   All data collected will remain confidential through the
and thought—thank you!...This class makes me feel slightly
following procedures:
inadequate.

i.   your name will NOT be used in the study or in any other
         I look at all of these wonderful brave works and I yearn
ii.   representation of the study
         to do something amazing.

iii.   all taped interviews and discussions will be destroyed at
        Anyway, other than a feeling of immense talentlessness
        the conclusion of the study.
        (isn't making up words fun?)
iv.   each participant will have the opportunity to review and
        I'm really enjoying this class. I can say that I have
        comment on the transcripts.
        been inspired to
v.   all data are restricted to the investigator and instructor
        write and think creatively...

2. You may refuse to participate or withdraw at any time, without
...I think I have done more writing in the last three weeks than I
prejudice, *even if you sign this letter of consent.*
did in all of my undergraduate degree.

3. At any stage of your involvement you may request clarification
It is very painful—I'm not used to it... The projects [assign-
on any issue regarding the project.
ments] are very inviting and intriguing.

4. This study will NOT involve any risk of any kind whatsoever.
I hope to take advantage to release myself from analytical
You will not be rewarded or penalized in any way for your
writing that I have been forced to adhere to for so long.
involvement (or lack of) in the study. Similarly, data collection
We'll see what happens and where it takes me...I have a
and analysis will in NO way affect the course grades of
story inside of me which must be written. I have
participating and non-participating students. All students will
been aware of it for years. I just never have the time. It's
receive the same instruction regardless of their involvement (or
been in my head and I need to tell
lack of) in the study.
it.

It is hoped that you will benefit from the interaction, reflection,
I would like to see more of how this is going to help us
and group and self-study. You will be given every opportunity

as teachers. I would love to get my students to write in
to provide input. In turn, I will provide ongoing feedback
class, but I don't get much of a chance in biology classrooms.
to participants as the study proceeds.
I guess I'll just have to try harder.

Further clarification regarding this project may be obtained from
...I haven't learned anything but we're being challenged to
Dr. Carl Leggo, Language Education (822 4040 Ponderosa E 215),
overlook our apprehensions and just express the way we feel. I
or from Gary Rasberry (739-6813, Ponderosa F 104). Please
like that. I think our time in this class has great potential for
indicate your consent to participate in Part Two of the study
growth...Unfortunately, sad as it is, I don't see myself being
by completing the form below and returning it to me. Thank
able to share [my writing]. I do, however, plan on continuing to
you for your willingness to participate.
write now that I realize I enjoy it.

I, _____ , have read
On my assignment, you gave me 17 out of 20—maybe you don't
the above and have had the opportunity to discuss in full the
know how difficult it is for me to write and share it with
nature of this project. I understand that my participation in this
someone. It just seems like I don't want to share it if you're
project, and the data collected, will be totally divorced from my
going to put a mark on it because it almost reinforces to me
assessment in ENED 426: Language Across the Curriculum. I
that I'm not much of a poet, at least not a 20 out of 20 poet.
understand that the entry of a researcher into my classroom will
I realize you can't give everyone a 20 out of 20, but if you're
be done as unobtrusively as possible, with minimum disruption of
giving 20 on the basis of how much heart went into it, I
normal classroom proceedings and in consultation with me.
put lots into it—21 worth...

I have had the opportunity to question both Dr. Carl Leggo
...A very purposeful emphasis on process. Where will it

and Mr. G. W. Rasberry. I give my consent to participate in this
go? I'm seeing poetry in everything: I think I will
project. I acknowledge receipt of a copy of this document.
write a poem...

Signed   _____

Dated   _____

CHAPTER ONE

Through a Poet's I

This book is about desire and daily life. I began it because I needed a way of thinking about poetry outside of writing poems...to imagine other ways of navigating into our collective future.

—Adrienne Rich, *What Is Found There*, 1993.

Desire and daily life: it would be difficult to imagine education in the absence of either. The tangle of lines and lives that run through this book would suggest that education is itself an imagining, a way of *navigating into our collective future*; and further, that poetry has something to do with this imagining, something to say about the ways that desire and daily life come together and apart as we spend our time engaged in acts of learning and teaching—of living in and outside of classrooms.

At the same time, poetry is itself a word that I am at times uneasy with. Reticent in certain kinds of ways to speak the word, fearing the worst from possible conversational outcomes: on buses, during family gatherings, at seminars and colloquia, in the gym. I am eager to reimagine the word poetry—particularly as I bring it to bear upon pedagogy. I am curious about the ways that my identity, personally and professionally, is (always being) carved, crafted, and shaped by words. By poetry. Similarly, I am curious about the ways my identity is always a result of my carving, my crafting, my shaping of words. Of poetry. I could speak in similar ways of my relations with pedagogy. I could place pedagogy in poetry's place and wonder over the similarities, the differences. Wonder over the ways in which my identity is about poetry and not about poetry, about pedagogy and not about pedagogy. Wonder over the ways my identity, like the identities of the teacher candidates I spend time with, engaged in acts of poetry and pedagogy, is shifting. Fleeting. In flux. Always.

In an odd sense, poetry is a word that has become somewhat worn out. Insisting on carrying everyone else's baggage, poetry sometimes struggles under the weight of its own history. Perhaps pedagogy, as a word, is no different. Not in the ways each of them mean but in the ways that they have both come to mean almost anything and/or everything to everyone. My own belief is that poetry is a way of imagining and reimagining words and worlds. I might say the same of pedagogy. There is a lot more to say about both. Poetry and pedagogy.

I have Adrienne Rich to thank, then, at the outset of this particular imagining for her offerings of a way to begin "thinking about poetry outside of writing poems." As Toronto artist Andy Patton (1995) has said about particular writers whose words he cherishes spending time with, Adrienne Rich, for me, is "a voice in which I've been soaking" (150) for a number of years.

Of particular value for me has been the ways in which Rich takes the poem and cracks it open into life, into the living. Takes it well beyond words on the page without ever losing sight of the sources from which the words grow. Her writing—of poems and of a living that includes the practice of writing poetry and living poetically—reminds me of a film I once saw in school called the *Powers of Ten*.[1] The memory, like the film, is old and plagued some by white spots and burn marks that scroll by as the spool engages, but I am remembering that the opening images depict two people sitting on a blanket on a lawn. The camera takes us, first, inward and inward and inward, until we are viewing these human beings at a cellular, then molecular, then submolecular level. The movement then reverses itself to take us outward, each movement in increments of powers of ten, until we are viewing human life and the earth from outer space,
and eventually, outer   outer space...
Finally, we are drawn earthward once again until
gravity rests
its case and we are bodily present,
grounded. Somehow
different. The universe seen through
a poet's I...

---

[1] I have since been able to locate the book, *Powers of Ten*, written by Philip and Phylis Morrison (1982), based on the brief and beautiful film *Powers of Ten: A Film Dealing with the Relative Size of Things in the Universe and the Effect of Adding Another Zero*, made by the Office of Charles and Ray Eames.

Adrienne Rich says,

> For a long time I've been trying to write poems as if, within this social order, it was enough to voice public pain, speak memory, set words in a countering order, call up images that were in danger of being forgotten or unconceived...But I've also lived with other voices whispering that poetry might be little more than self-indulgence in a society so howling with unmet human needs...It's been possible to consider poetry as a marginal activity, of passionate concern to its practitioners perhaps, but as specialized, having little to do with common emergency, as fly-fishing. (1993, 18)

I, too, hear the "other voices whispering." Some years ago, as this book, this imagining, was just beginning to take shape I was working on a poem. The opening line read, *Eye seem to have a poet's I*. It felt like a wonderful opening, but the pen couldn't seem to move fast enough before the opening closed. The poem remains unfinished still, not for lack of words or feelings about what it might mean to have a poet's I, but possibly because it was never meant to end. The poem's opening stanzas look something like this:

Eye seem to have a poet's I,
not for any particular rhyme   or reason.

Maybe it's just because
I have always been

will always be
un   finished.

Uncomfortable in happiness
incomplete in unhappiness

insecure in outwardness
confident in   introspection...

The middle stanzas, which I have left out in this particular rendering, stumble self-reflexively in search of some invisible pattern, scratch at metaphysical quandaries, mix metaphors of mining and writing with pickaxe determination, stretch toward quiddity (a useful word for poets and pedagogues), and then look for a soft place to land. As the final stanza picks itself up

off the floor, a question surfaces,
dust-covered: *What good the poet's I?*
at which point, a shaky
scratch-and-claw voice approximating my own
drops deep deeper
into steep-shaft darkness
knowing the poet's I
with less certainty
than eye could ever have
imagined.

This poetic anecdote is a way of saying that I relate to Rich's thoughts on poetry-as-fly-fishing, just as I relate to her sense of the urgency and importance of poetry—poetry that exists outside of writing poems. In fact, one of poetry's many possibilities might even lie in its capacity to bring fly-fishing and *unmet human needs* together. Not for the purpose of jest or satire or "Far Side(d)" humor, but for the ways that language can sometimes make us different for having tried. For allowing language to *pierce the routines*. For entertaining the possibility of the Strange in the Familiar. And for allowing the Familiar to appear Strange. Contradictions. Juxtapositions. Combinations. Permutations. Desire and daily life. Writing and research. Poetry and pedagogy.

In addressing the work of the poet, Don McKay makes a distinction between "poetic attention and romantic inspiration" (1995, 24). (In hindsight, I think it's the romantic inspiration aspect of poetry that I am quick to deny possession of in pedagogical circles, then give myself away, of course, in self[conscious] defense.) And while I must acknowledge the romantic pull of the poet's I in my writing (which includes poetry), I am interested in the ways McKay's description of poetic attention—as a "form of knowing" in which language acknowledges itself—might inform my writing of research: As artifice, as essential, as inadequate, as impossible, as necessary. As McKay offers,

> Language is experiencing its speechlessness and the consequent need to stretch *itself* to be adequate to this form of knowing...the persistence of poetic attention during the act of composition is akin to the translator's attention to the original, all the while she performs upon it a delicate and dangerous transformation. Our epistemological dilemma is not resolved ...but ritualized and explored. (1995, 26)

Poetry outside of writing poems, then, has something to say about lines *and* lives; it has something to say about research. Poetry, like pedagogy and our research of pedagogy, is akin to translation. As Andy Patton (1995) suggests, "it's not poetry [and, I would add, pedagogy] that we study but its translation into other words" (155). This kind of poetic attention to language, as a research sensibility, refuses opposites, resists dichotomies. Research through a poet's I does not necessarily beg for phenomenological brushstrokes that paint portraits of our teaching and learning in true, living color, but neither does it call for postmodern pastiche, a beautifully meaningless collage of human experience.

Somewhere in-between, the poet Bronwen Wallace, echoed by the hermeneutic research of David Jardine (1992a, 1992b, 1992c, 1993, 1994a, 1994b, 1995a, 1995b), makes an (interpretive) case for "the stubborn argument of the particular"(Wallace 1987, 111). As Jardine notes, "only through a deliberate and disciplined attention to the stubborn particulars is the whole anything more than simply a floating, and, in the end, unsustainable idea" (Jardine 1995a, 272). And, significantly, there is both "multiplicity and particularity [in] the local" (Hutcheon 1992, 13).

In turn, I ask, what is it about the particulars of our learning—our writing and reading and teaching and living—that remain so "stubborn" to our writing and reading and teaching and living—to our researching? How is it that our pedagogical relations with these "stubborn particulars" can bear the tension of both invitation and resistance? And, what kinds of conditions for teachers and learners and/or for writers and researchers might we create in order to savor and celebrate, problematize, and trouble over the "stubborn particulars" of writing and reading? Teaching and learning? Research?

This book attempts to dwell with/in this tension, this language of invitation and resistance. It attempts to create an interpretive location somewhere between poetry and pedagogy. And research. It attempts to live well with/in the tangle of writing and teaching and reading and learning and living and researching, of methodology and epistemology. It attempts to honor the importance of the stubborn particular that comes out of attending to the lines and the lives, as Bronwen Wallace says, the "right now, in the midst of things, *this* and *this*" (1987, 111). The book attempts also to imagine research as an imagining that sometimes strays far from the living, cuts itself off from the living in order to write about it. It attempts to live on "the hinge of translation" (McKay 1995, 28). Through a poet's I. Writing research. Researching writing.

Adrienne Rich says, "When I can pull it together, I work in solitude surrounded by community, solitude in dialogue with community, solitude that alternates with collective work" (1993, 53). Not only the poet's I. But also poets' I's. Most times, this book is their I's through my eyes. Their eyes through my I's. A danger, of course. A risk. Delicate and dangerous. Like teaching. Like learning. Like writing. Like research. Like life.

In a poignant and self-reflexive turn, feminist educator and filmmaker Trinh T. Minh-ha states, "I write to show myself showing people who show me my own showing" (1989, 22). Her words offer another way to begin to describe the nature of the work of this book which attempts to live well with the relationships among literacy, aesthetic practice, and the ongoing production of subjectivity. Trinh T. Minh-ha's writings speak particularly well to poststructural understandings of the experience of identity that are carved out of the complexities of language. Writing (and) identity are the infinite play of empty mirrors, writes Minh-ha, an ongoing play that reveals our doubles, our ghosts, our flaws, our imperfections. In this way, my own writing (self) suffers under the spell of such narcissistic tensions, even as it attempts to catch the reflections of other selves' writing: "rare are the moments when we accept leaving our mirrors empty" (1989, 22).

While necessarily caught up in the illusory nature of trying to write the real, I attempt, still, to portray some of the ways in which a life that includes writing—or, a study of a self, studying education—is deeply implicated in other lives that include writing, other selves, studying education (Britzman and Pitt 1996; Sumara 1996a). Within the limited humility that writing a life—or lives—offers, I look to Minh-ha's offering of a more generous interpretation of writing a life, in which a self-study is not *only* a self-study

> For writing, like a game that defies its own rules, is an ongoing practice that may be said to be concerned, not with inserting a 'me' into language, but with creating an opening where the 'me' disappears while 'I' endlessly come and go, as the nature of language requires. (1989, 35)

"What is the experience of living a life that includes the practice of writing?" This question permeates the next chapter, "A Bowl of Yellow Flowers Stains the Canvas"—so much so that it becomes invisible in its persistence. Chapter 2 is, in many ways, a "sampler" in the postmodern sense in which Linda Hutcheon (1992) uses the term to refer to a "kind of formal sampling or self-reflexive, parodic manipulation"(10) of text..."the 'sampler' erodes the tried and true...distinction between original and copy" (Hutcheon 1992, 9). "A Bowl of Yellow Flowers" is a story within a story within a story; it is a part of the whole. A whole in part. Chapter 2 is (in) the book. The book is (in) chapter 2. It re-presents an attempt at (the) writing out (of) an experience(ing) of a life that includes writing as it writes its way into and out of the necessary tangle of teachers' lives that also include the practice of writing and teaching and learning.

Chapter 3,"A Life That Includes Writing," is an attempt to sketch some of the lines and lives by moving in and around the classroom experience of teacher candidates who explored writing pedagogy and teacher education in a writing workshop-styled setting. The workshop offered opportunities for teacher candidates to begin viewing writing practice as a curricular form that enabled possibilities for further writing practice. The chapter attempts to show how, in the context of teacher education, writing practice, that includes "wordmaking" and "wordplay," becomes a way of *writing* practice—in order to discover our selves—to see our selves thinking out loud on paper in a (writing) process and practice that, like the process of learning itself, is interminable. In short, chapter 3 suggests that a life that includes writing must include a lot of writing (practice).

Chapters 4 and 5 offer a "trip through the tangle"—in theory and practice—on the way to chapter 6, the "concluding" chapter. These chapters re-present and enact a sometimes-stumbling-toward-meaning, what Shoshana Felman (1987) has called "the lived experience of a discovery," as the book dwells in the location of the workshop, a place of writing and teaching, in which the living and writing, the lines and the lives, become blurred. Teacher candidates negotiate the fixity and flux of the liminal space of student-teacher through writing. How might identity be negotiated through writing? Perhaps through writing, or *throughwriting*: on the way through to somewhere else...

Chapter 4, "Through the Tangle," lives with and through the question posed by Deborah Britzman and Alice Pitt (1996): "Can a study of the self, studying education create new conditions of learning and the making of pedagogical insight?" This chapter offers a tentative fulcrum, a state of im/balance, a place from which to experience the moment arm of the book move through its own series of shifting identity negotiations—from a self, studying education, to a self studying selves studying education. "The tangle," refracted through hermeneutics, postmodernism, psychoanalytic theory, writing practice, and pedagogy, is itself a location in which to situate a particular classroom practice, self-reflexively "learning to look closely into the dense particularities of concrete situations of teaching and learning" (Lather and Ellsworth 1996, 70).

Chapter 5, "The Curious Time of Researching Pedagogy," is a poetic attempt to imagine time in teacher education as something "other." It is an attempt to imagine the time of teacher education as an imagining that is itself tangled. Playing on Deborah Britzman's (1998) conceptualizations of "the curious time of pedagogy," this chapter (re)considers the curious time of *researching* pedagogy. The poet's I returns to what I have referred to as the "Small Imaginings" introduced in chapter 2 for the ways they create a location of ambivalence that enables me to cast the time of research—the time of learning—backward and forward

(Britzman and Pitt 1996) in order to complicate the practice of *writing* research and pedagogy.

Chapter 6: Teachers' writing lives, or, teachers writing (their) lives in ways that become teachers *writing* lives. This play on words is also the play of pedagogy, "a pedagogy that attempts to make space for students to 'perform differently'" (Orner 1996, 77). This chapter gives shape to a curricular location that offers the possibility of "work-shopping" and "word-shopping," both part of a playful process of ongoing identity negotiation through a writing practice that includes "wordmaking" and "wordplay." Word-shopping and work-shopping: in each case the hyphen introduces a space—re-members the space—as a location where teacher candidates can try on *both* lines and lives in a living that includes the practice of writing, as well as a practice that includes the writing of living. Through writing practice. Through *writing* practice. And through writing theory. Through *writing* theory. *Writing* practice into theory into practice. Teachers *writing* lives as a never ending process of learning to live "un/grammatically" (Leggo 1998).

* * *

What good the poet's I? (Re)Turning (to) the words of Adrienne Rich, this book "is about desire and daily life. I began it because I needed a way of thinking about poetry outside of writing poems...to imagine other ways of navigating into our collective future."

Now that I have rediscovered the power of *The Powers of Ten*, I find myself visiting and revisiting the marvel of words and images, the science and poetry of the universe contained on those pages, where both inner and outer are space. Out of the boggling array of fact and fancy, several small passages struck me in particular and I recount them here. First, in the book's introductory notes,

> The step-by-step examination within these pages is best shared by a traveler who is pleased alike by unexpected familiarity and by exotic novelty...

and then, later on,

These microscopic scenes are so near the edge of ordinary vision that they are recognized even in novelty, hidden surprises within the commonplace... [2]

Both the film and the book on which it is based create an awesome and impressive interpretive location from which to address questions that elude even our imagining. On one particular page of *Powers of Ten*, we are offered (an imagining?) of the skin of a human being at 10^{-4} meters. The caption below the grainystrange image reads,

Unexpected detail appears; we can scarcely orient ourselves. Deeper still, we enter an intimate world within, as unfamiliar to us as the distant stars.

The moments and movements of this book, this particular imagining—of the curious time of researching pedagogy—now seem suddenly small and insignificant against the weave of the cosmos. Still, it is easy to become lost in a life that includes writing, a life that includes imagining. There have been, and continue to be, many places in this text, in this curious time, where I can scarcely orient myself. My self. My selves. Yet, always, there is

"Unexpected familiarity...
Hidden surprises within the   commonplace."

Finally, then, moving from
an imagining of The Universe
to the tiny arrow that says,
You Are Here,
"these pages"—this imagining
is best shared by a traveler who is pleased alike by the
un   familiar.
writing research
         researching writing
         through a poet's I...

---

[2] There are no page numbers in the text.

a very large footnote with an
"I"
for form

_____ INTERLUDE

This book has been influenced by an issue of *Theory into Practice* called "Situated Pedagogies: Classroom Practices in Postmodern Times" (Lather and Ellsworth 1996). Each of the essays contributes to the conversation around what it might mean to live and teach within "the postmodern moment...sense made here is limited, local, provisional, and always critical" (Brenda Marshall, in Schaafsma 1996, 115). While many of the authors offer examples of students' writing, it interests me that Elizabeth Ellsworth chose not to include any "excerpts" of student words. The other authors go to great lengths to carefully cut and paste student comments into their texts, making sure not to take textual liberties under the constant and watchful eye of liberatory pedagogical research and practice. The eye, of course, is their own "I" which must learn to live self-reflexively within the potentially contradictory textual world that threatens to prescribe or reinscribe the very practices that seek to act as helpfully critical or emancipatory in the first place.

> I find the absence of student words/works in Ellsworth's representation of her classroom practice no less "real" for the lives that are apparently "missing." In fact, I find her account of classroom living to be entirely consistent with her efforts to become more and more "response-able" to the students and the relationships they share together in that commonplace location. This *is* part of the postmodern moment; their presence is, for me, made more real by their absence. As Ellsworth says, paraphrasing Rooney: there are no "innocent readings of the world" (1996, 138). Our readings of the world, or text, or curriculum, Ellsworth continues, are "neither possible nor impossible, but practical under certain political and theoretical conditions" (Ellen Rooney, in Ellsworth, 138). I read Ellsworth (and Rooney 1989) for the helpful ways in which they make explicit the conditions of production in their curricular work.

I, too, seek ways to make my curricular workings of the text more explicit and choose to represent the living and writing practices of the preservice teachers as a series of constructions, a textual strategy subject to a reading that is co-produced—performed—through the conscious and unconscious exclusions and omissions of reader and writer. I seek to create forms for my writing of the preservice teachers' writings, comments, and questionings that foreground their textual performance as staged excerpts. I offer poetry and anecdotal comments in the form of "interludes" as Mary Aswell Doll has employed them—parenthetical placements between the "important moments of a lived life" (1995, vii). The interludes also appear as footnotes and as poetry, as fractured tales and unfinished business. Other textual additions in the body of the book include student comments from e-mail messages and "exit slips."

CHAPTER TWO

A Bowl of Yellow Flowers Stains the Canvas

One of the central concerns of hermeneutics, and one of the reasons for a cyclical mode of inquiry, is the question of how one might go about inquiring into a phenomenon in which one is immersed, entangled, and complicit.

—Brent Davis, *Teaching Mathematics*, 1996.

Something About This Wall: An Opening Prelude

Here is a broad stone wall flicking alive small green flames of lizards. The wall is low: I sit on its back watching the road that curves around the wet blue belly of the sea... [1]

Already there is something about this wall, something about this orderly collection of stone that demands patience and curiosity. I cannot yet say what this something is, though I am compelled to wait here for some kind of unfolding. Maybe it's only the promise of a story that holds me in place, a deliberate building with words—word upon word upon word—that makes the road worth watching; this *road that curves around the wet blue belly of the sea.*

The sea is always itself, restless, forever altering its colours like a sad eye; the road itself never shifts; the squat wall I balance on is like the tough arm of an old fisherman. It keeps children and old women from dancing off the cliffs.

---

[1] These opening lines of Connelly's "A Bowl of Yellow Flowers Stains the Canvas" paint a scene that opens out into a story which haunts the work of this chapter. Connelly's words are italicized throughout the haunting, while my own remain in plain font. I am grateful to Karen Connelly—for her words, her poetry, her stories.

Blindly With Words:
Introductory Notes on Ambiguity, Self-Reflexivity, and Desire

> Painting is trying to paint what you cannot paint and writing is what
> you cannot know before you have written: it is preknowing and not
> knowing, blindly with words. (Cixous 1993, 38)

Blindly with words. This is my hope-full intention, my strategic desire: to move forward with words, one word at a time, surrounded by the words of so many others, others whose words create "a weave of knowing and not-knowing which is what knowing is" (Spivak, in Lather 1991, 49). I feel very much a part of this weave as I begin to gather words: borrowing, sorting, presenting, and re-presenting. As such, I am committed in satisfyingly obsessive ways to inventing and reinventing the answers that question what research is and quite willing to embrace the ambiguity and uncertainty involved in such a pursuit "given the postmodern foregrounding of the ways we create our worlds via language" (Lather 1991, 14). If, indeed, we only see the world we make, then we must be prepared for our world(s) to be full of problem and possibility, alive with interpretability (Jardine 1995a).

This commitment to obsession is why I choose to begin this waterfall of words with the kind of existential dilemma that Cixous invites us to consider for our own lives: is it fear or desire (or perhaps fear of desire) that compels us to put one word after another in order to compose our selves and our living? Blindly with words. Now, one might choose to argue with Cixous over her choice of the word "blindly," feeling it is perhaps too heavy a word, too overstated for the task of our work as curricular artists who seek to invent and reinvent ourselves in "the language of the world where we all live and work" (Grumet 1988, xviii). Still, for me and for the spirit of the work I wish to pursue on this particular journey, the imagery of Cixous's canvas holds an important tension, "an unsettling juxtaposition of opposites" (Moore, in Hillman 1989) that I believe we must learn to live well with. Preknowing and not knowing.

If not blindly, there is certainly a (hermeneutic) sense in which the painter or poet, the writer or researcher works with/in a series of difficult and dedicated movements, a sometimes-stumbling

toward meaning, "endeavoring to render visible that which has become invisible" (Sumara 1996a, 120). As Brent Davis (1996) so beautifully offers, "I do not seek a blind pedagogy, nor do I believe that teaching is currently deaf. Rather, the quest is for a middle way" (xxiv). In the hermeneutic tradition, it is this middle way I choose to travel, entertaining both a crazy optimism that anticipates "the suddenly kindled light of the never-before-said" (Kundera 1986, 123) as well as a sober respect for the impossibility of language that "disrupts, refuses to be contained with boundaries" (hooks 1994, 167). In the midst of this hour-glassed living, our research slipping
through the eye
of a storm, we must
at times be compelled to walk
slowly feel the pull
of the earth the beating
of our hearts beneath
our skin, breath short and   choppy.

Perhaps
we should fall on our hands
and knees crawl
across sun-streaked pavement kiss
the cracks, notice the beautiful
imperfection of   everything.

For so long we have scratched and
clawed like ravens, like blind
dogs, children waking
in sun-darkened caves
filled with passageways and possibilities
and always dark light
at the end of the tunnel.

But now we are lizards
all scales and eyes unblinking
part way up the wall, warmed
by the sun.

Aware.
Unmoving.

We speak in tongues
having crossed the desert and become
grains of sand,
there is nothing left
to tell.

Yet, tell we must, and this is how it must begin—like art, like poetry, like curriculum—waiting for the world to imagine itself out of a seed, or run its course like an avalanche down a garden path, ripping up color as it goes. And so the work that follows dreams (of) poetry and pedagogy, curriculum and the "hermeneutic imagination" (Smith 1994), writing (and) research, teacher education and everydayness.

My initial intent was to research "the writing life"—to explore writing theory and pedagogy and the living that such practice and theory requires. I am now discovering that my desire is also to write the research(ing) life, where "writing is not just a mopping-up activity at the end of a research project...[it] is also a way of 'knowing'...a method of inquiry" (Richardson 1994, 516). Concomitant with this project is the desire to celebrate and interrogate "a language [and a living] that lives beneath our desires for fixity and clarity and centration" (Jardine 1994a, 512).

My reasons for "choosing" difficulty do not spring from some romantic or altruistic notion that the best research can only come from selfless dedication and sacrifice; they are more the result of discovering and acknowledging "the value in dedicating ourselves to the difficulty of *not knowing* where our engagement with the text [or canvas] [might] lead" (Sumara 1996a, 147). As Lorri Neilsen suggests, "It is not an easy place to be, but it is alive" (1998, 182). As such, it is an invitation
of sorts, to consider both
the writing and the living
as though they were so many colors in search
of a palette. And the dream
is the canvas.
And painting is trying to paint

what you cannot
paint.
And, of course,
through it all
there is   *a broad stone wall*
flicking alive small green flames of lizards…

The Writing(s) on the Wall: A Traveller's (Foot) Note

The pilgrimage is not one of place…The pilgrimage is one of spirit, and if that spirit allows no rest, no steady rhythm, no resolution of form or content, it is because [*the broad stone wall, writing and researching, and a bowl of yellow flowers*] live a life of their own and ceaselessly haunt my work. (Livingston 1990, vii)

No rest, no steady rhythm, no resolution of form: *The sea is always itself, restless, forever altering its colours like a sad eye…*Myra Cohn Livingston says that "poets need readers, just as they need the world around them" (1990, 20). In the same breath, she refers to Robert Frost, who speaks of a "right reader." While I agree wholeheartedly with the idea that poets (and writers of all flights and fancy) need a world and/of readers, with all due respect to Frost, I am not certain there is such a thing as a "right reader"; it seems to fly in the face of Barthes's notion of a writerly text which invites the reader not to be right, but to write the text in a way that may or may not be "right." (Or, as one reader of this text has suggested, "Maybe a 'write reader' would be preferable.")

As readers and writers, then, we are responsible in our own ways for acknowledging what David Jardine refers to as the "helplessness and weakness of the written word [which] is also its strength, for in such weakness, writing retains an irreducible 'porousness' and 'openness'" (1992a, xx). This seems another way of saying that as much as we desire to invest our words with certain meaning(s) and, in turn, to give them over to the world in a way that our meaning might be received, we are, in the end, not entirely in charge of the proceedings. This is not to say that since we can't be sure what meaning(s) readers will make with our words then we are not responsible for our author-ity; rather, part of our responsibility lies in remaining open to the possibility of multiple meanings and, in turn, being prepared to live well with both the satisfaction as well as the difficulty of potential mis/understandings that may arise in the face of such multiplicity. This "learning to live well" with/in our relations, textual and otherwise, has implications for teaching and learning and for the shared experience of living a life that includes reading and writing. This particular section, then, subtitled "A Traveller's (Foot) Note," represents my initial attempt to navigate and negotiate pathways of meaning with other readers/writers as I/we begin to wonder in a sustained way about the relationships we create and enact when immersing ourselves in (curricular) acts of reading/writing.

This chapter exists on canvas, though as art/ifice it is part of "a laying open of possibilities that suspends any final completion" (Greene 1994, 213). As my writings began to grow into something that might be recognized as a book, my "painting" was a *trying to paint* (what I could not paint). I experimented. Created. Invented rituals—whispered incantations, walked around the canvas *three times counterclockwise for luck and momentum (putting the hex on cliché)*:

> Prussian blue [was] the colour on the tip of the brush. There [was] a stroke to make. [My] hand move[d] forward and then [it] stop[ped]. The instant that connect[ed] wishing and doing, linking movement of a hand from palette to brush to canvas, began to vibrate like a thread under tension. The thread glisten[ed], hummed as it [was] pulled. (Ignatieff 1993, 33)

Then—*out of the blue*—words fell on open fields, planted themselves. I became immersed in not-knowing as a way toward meaning, quite confident in my uncertainty and quite enthusiastic about inviting others to join me in that cloud of unknowing. Yet, as an aspiring artist, as a reader and writer and researcher, self-reflexivity most often shows myself to me in images of self-effacing clarity: watching myself watch myself—sometimes splashing the canvas with colors I've never even seen before, dreaming abstract as I paint-by-number. It is not long before I am splashing my contradictions all about. I tend a careful garden, longing for dark coastal forests where hungry green continues to invent itself: crazily.

With the first writing of this painting, I followed myself wherever I wanted to go. No rest, no steady rhythm, no resolution of form: *The sea is always itself, restless, forever altering its colours like a sad eye.* Then, after the courage that was also an unveiling, I invited others to come with me to the sea. Many felt the waves as I had, others watched from the wall. Others wished the wall was a little higher, a little lower, wanted a different view, thought the ocean could not possibly come in those colors. I wished they could see my ocean, wished they could understand my place on the wall. Wished they could be the right readers. In the end, however, as Michael Ignatieff (1993) notes in his book *Scar Tissue*, "there is almost nothing a person will not do in order to be understood. They will even pull their life apart so that what was not understood can at last be seen, like a wound" (114). I grew uneasy with the first whispers of (possible) mis-understanding and began to backtrack, then unravel my text in order to show it to others more clearly, assure them—but mostly myself—that my intentions were epistemologically sound. Look! I pleaded, it's right here between the lines.

Having mostly re-covered from those earlier experiences of dis-comfort, with the best of intentions, I attempt now to find a middle way, not so that I might be a servant to understanding, and not only for the reader but also for myself—for us—so that together we might stumble contentedly between our uneasy desire to honor Mystery and our insatiable need to understand. In so doing, I hope to play with/in the im/possible tension required of our living well together—of our painting and reading and writing. And researching.

In our textual dwelling together, it is often form that provides the underpinnings of our coming together and coming apart. Sometimes this shaping and creating, this unfolding of form is an ecological movement—a deepening—*waiting for the moon to find a form that signals the planet's giving way to an inevitable shade born out of light.* In such an unfolding, form is not necessarily ours to manage, but rather something that we are always and already a part of; shaping as we are shaped; it is the momentary loss of breath that comes with the sudden shock of recognition at seeing form reveal itself to us as we work/sculpt/write/paint—as we re-search. Sometimes form is a transcendence through the simple movement of breath; it is the semicolon that says "Wait here for just a moment," or the hyphen with its invitation into a space/place of ambiguity: as barrier, as breath, as tightrope, as pregnant pause. It could also be the diagonal stroke (/) "that within its slant is already inscribed living tension" (Aoki 1997). These are the placements of words and symbols that mark our lives and become "announcements in the language that dreams speak"(Lineham 1995). Sometimes form is the geography, geomorphology even, of the text, the sliding of textual plates, the formation of paragraphs and poetry, that allow us to "lay down a path while walking"[2]—allow us to discover the lay of the land. Very often, however, we do not allow for form's complexity, forget to account for form in our textual living. As Dennis Sumara (1996a) states, "Although modern readers want to be surprised, they want the surprise to be an unexpected event, not an unorthodox structure" (151). As a poet, who is also a teacher, I am most often drawn, in my own reading and writing, to surprise—to "the mystery which withdraws, which never hands itself over in a form we can trust" (Caputo 1987, 270). Expecting always the unexpected. I relish the prospects of becoming lost in the (textual) world. As a teacher who is also a poet, I feel it is, at the same time, important to acknowledge and honor the relationality of our textual travels together, feel it is important to establish some kind of "map of pedagogical responsibility" (Sumara 1996a, 141) with those whom I share my writing and reading, teaching and learning so that we might find our way (or get lost) together. It is a map that speaks of a commitment and a certain obligation, a "co-laboring" that says that "somehow the personal and the communal must co-exist" (Sumara 1996a, 143). It is a map that when read, finds me sincere and sensitive: "This is a favorite of mine that I want to share with you...Please listen attentively! It's important to me that you read carefully" (Sumara 1996a, 157). In turn I will respect and care for your reading(s) that make my writing(s) possible. It is a map that finds me parodic and playful: "Throw away the map if you like, just take a *wander for wonder's*

---

[2] I was introduced to Franciso Varela's notion of "laying down a path in walking" by Sumara (1996a, 127, 175), and by Davis (1996, 40, 79, 129).

sake."[3] It is a map that finds me eager and enthusiastic: "Just read me!" This introductory section and the section that follows (see "Blind Spots and Irrelevant Adumbrations") are, as promised then, an explanatory offering based on the fan/observer's historic complaint—and the vendor's familiar refrain—that "you can't tell the players without a program." I offer them as a set of postmodern program notes, as a guide for a particular piece of writing that, at times, may take both reader and writer "under" for sustained periods without coming up for breath as it willingly and unwillingly blurs the lines around whose story is being told and who is actually doing the telling. The idea for a "guide" was prompted by some who have read this work and suggested that an introduction or commentary might be useful in helping readers read the piece:

> With experimental writing[4] it's always hard to know if what seems difficult or exceptional is intentional or if it could be usefully revised to help the reader along...The piece is interesting but makes me feel like I need the author along, sitting on the wall, talking me through this.[5]

So, realizing that "having the author along" for the journey is neither feasible nor desirable, and having long given up on the idea of a right reader, I offer instead an age-old curricular nemesis, the antithesis of art, a multiple choice in order to assist the traveller as the journey begins...

a) Read the following section—"Blind Spots and Irrelevant Adumbrations"—as one would a set of program notes before proceeding to the main body of the text.

---

[3] "Wander for wonder" is the name of a particular writing exercise used during the course (see chapter 6).

[4] Unlike the reviewer of my work who is quoted above, I am somewhat reticent to call my own writing "experimental" feeling just a bit presumptuous in that (self) labelling. It helps (me), however, to refer to Laurel Richardson's use of the term *experimental representations* in "Writing: A method of inquiry." In N. Denzin and Y. Lincoln (Eds.), *Handbook of qualitative research,* 520–521.

[5] This comment came from a reviewer who read an earlier version of this chapter for *Writing on the Edge,* a journal based at the University of California at Davis.

b) Bypass the following section and wade directly into the body of the text—(Already) (There is) Something About This Wall: An Unfolding—and become willing participants with/in an "ideology of doubt" (Richardson 1994, 520).

c) Some of the above

d) None of the above

e) Read/Write/Read the text in whatever way you see fit.

"Blind Spots and Irrelevant Adumbrations": A Traveller's Guide

Here is a broad stone wall flicking alive small green flames of lizards. The wall is low: I sit on its back watching the road that curves around the wet blue belly of the sea.

These are the words of poet and writer Karen Connelly (1993) as she begins to carve *A Bowl of Yellow Flowers Stains the Canvas,* a beauty-filled short story. A poem, really. A piece of non?fiction. The sea and the (broad stone) wall that affords its view—as you will soon see—become constants as they mark a scene that shifts, sometimes imperceptibly, sometimes dramatically around them. With words, exquisite and polished, we are offered an intimate view, a meditation—through a(nother) Poet's I—of an extra-ordinary series of events.

Watching the road that curves around the wet blue belly of the sea, it is easy to forget everything else and simply surrender to the steady breathing of wave upon wave. This is a perfectly acceptable option, to be pulled by storyline and tide. The Poet's I is playful and inviting: "We are charmed out of the ordinary by the riches of words" (Hillman 1992, 155). But as the story proceeds, there is a growing sense of dis-ease amid the charm, an uncertainty as to whose story is being told and by whom—a result not only of Connelly's intricate literary weavings that begin to grow tendril-like around the unfolding scene, but also due to the addition of my writings/readings which sometimes blend with and at other times disrupt the ongoing narrative.

Following Jacques Daignault,[6] I am "entering the *Literary Space*...welcoming words, welcoming characters, welcoming emotions, welcoming the imaginary...giving up ideas but not completely." In seeking to be part of Connelly's work, I am opening myself to what the literary space might have to say to my researcherly imagination. (As Daignault says, sometimes our research is "too real.") And so together Connelly and I invent/re-invent, present/re-present *real*, separated only by the thin skin of convention: her breath *italicized* and then frozen as font, my own breath "un-italicized," as though I assume the reader might believe I have some textual right to a place (t)here between the lines in the first place.

And there are the voices of others still, others whose words become part of the weave in ways that belie the apparent seamlessness of the text. In bringing the scholarly world of educational research with me, I am entering and embracing Daignault's "*Intertextual Space*...welcoming influences... acknowledging and thanking all those I need to thank...welcoming others" (who are not really Other): Madeleine Grumet, Jeanette Winterson, John Caputo, David Smith, Dennis Sumara, David Jardine, bell hooks, Brent Davis, Deborah Britzman, Hélène Cixous, to name but a few.

I may have, at various points during the process of writing, tried consciously or otherwise, to deny my role in this orchestrated heteroglossia. Karen Connelly has, after all, consented to my request to "use" her poetic text for my academic experimentations.[7] In turn, I have followed accepted conventions

---

[6] The notion of "literary space" re-presented here comes from a talk Jacques Daignault gave at the Faculty of Education, The University of British Columbia, February 27, 1996. I am grateful for the opportunities I have had to talk and listen with Jacques, in classrooms and cafés, over the course of his sabbatical year in Vancouver.

[7] In what could only be a literary-fuelled event—'non' and 'fiction' twisting and turning with one another in a strong ocean breeze—I wrote Karen to ask permission to use her story. (I had heard that she was not enthusiastic toward the APA-formatted world of the Academy.) Some weeks later, a postcard found its way through my mailslot from a small Greek Island with Karen's blessing and encouragement for my work. A shaky correspondence with Karen

in "using" the texts of others—academic or otherwise—careful always to indent here, cite there, leaving a trail of institutionally recognizable crumbs as I go. Still there is a sense in which I have bent and twisted the words of others to suit my own intentions and sensibilities. It is to Bakhtin's (1981) sense of contestation and seizure and appropriation—in which "many words stubbornly resist, others remain alien, sound foreign in the mouth of the one who appropriated them and who now speaks them" (294)—that I refer. My willingness to embrace a kind of cacophony of voices and stir them up in order to celebrate the embedded and multiple soundings of many suggests a certain kind of postmodern sensibility that aspires to open up rather than close off possibility. Even so, still in play are my ever-present feelings of dis-ease at playing writer or researcher as "ventriloquist,"[8] belying the difficulties and problematics of having others speak through/for me.

Though the wall and the constant interplay of I's may raise difficult questions for many—cause consternation even—many still will choose to follow the "magic thread" it weaves: "It pierces and runs through our hearts"(Connelly 1995, 15). As Richardson (1994) says, experimental writers work within an "ideology of doubt" and raise a number of important questions,

> questions of how the author positions the Self as a knower and a teller...these lead to the intertwined problems of subjectivity/ authority/ authorship/ reflexivity, on the one hand, and representational form, on the other. (1994, 520)

---

ensued—postcards being the wordcarrier-of-choice as my paper moved through to its eventual conclusion (which, as it turns out, was not really a conclusion at all).

[8] I am indebted to Lorri Neilsen and her work at Mount Saint Vincent University. Several years ago she introduced me to the notion of "researcher-as-ventriloquist" and we continue to discuss its ramifications for our lives as teachers and re-searchers and poets. Following Neilsen, I believe that this dis-ease is part and parcel of writing and researching; rather than avoiding it, the task is ours, as researchers, to address it continually through self-reflexive positionings that point to ourselves as we point to the world. (Lather's *Getting Smart* remains an excellent re-source for who seek to live well with this type of dis-ease.)

Working with/in Connelly's (and others') text(s) allows me to experiment with these different sets of I's, to employ forms of writing that Richardson (1994) calls "evocative representations":

> Trying out evocative forms, we relate differently to our material; we know it differently. We find ourselves attending to feelings, ambiguities, temporal sequences, blurred experiences...we struggle to find a textual place for ourselves and our doubts and uncertainties. (521)

My own 'I' finds its way into Connelly's text, not with explicitly confounding intentions, but aware nonetheless of the possibility for increased complexity, confusion even. Together, our I's are not only self-reflexive—playful or parodic in their concern for language and the manipulation of text—they are also privileged eyes from scene to shining scene. From the wall, the poet narrates, feigns omniscience, doles the scene out in bits and pieces of her choosing according to an internal (and often hidden agenda.) In turn, I employ many of the same strategies. The wall thus becomes a place from which not only to witness but also to question the unfolding scene, construct it, even; it is (t)here I seek to find my own place in the tangle, relishing the view, disrupting the view, playing with the colors the ocean makes possible.

In her more recent work, *One Room in a Castle*, Karen Connelly (1995) begins to ponder—then play—with many of the conventional boundaries we have scratched in the sand to separate (and confound) 'non' and 'fiction': "Why create another story when so many are being lived?" she asks, poking (fun) at the storymaking machine which creates its own fascinating criteria for what is real/fiction. This is wonderfully dangerous territory to explore, and Connelly is only one of many who choose to work with/on "the rough edges of our crisp categories...the gaps in our precise definitions (Davis 1996, 14).[9] Wonderfully dangerous because many (readers/writers) want to have their (non)(fiction) and read/write it too. While many wade into the textual fray, willingly suspending all judgment; others do not want their trust

---

[9] For those interested in the playful and parodic treatment of language and literary genres, I recommend a collection of short "fiction" titled *Likely Stories: A PostmodernSampler*, edited by George Bowering and Linda Hutcheon.

betrayed. This hearkens back to my earlier discussion (in "A Traveller's (Foot) Note") of form out of which so many of our historical reading/writing habits and traditions are born/constructed. While many writers may attempt to use form to organize/construct the relations between and among the text and reader and writer, they may also use form to dis-organize and dis-orient, to deconstruct these relations. Dennis Sumara, however, asks us to consider not only the form, but our naming of that form. He notes, for example, that when we choose to name something as fiction then culturally we know how to engage with it. (Even if/when that engagement sometimes involves the acceptance of not knowing how to engage with a particular text/fiction.) Difficulties arise, however, when some of our con/textual clues are strategically veiled or buried or hidden; therefore, it's not so much the form but how it's "announced." As Sumara (1995) states, this naming-of-things in our literary and curricular lives (and imaginations) needs to be interrogated in an interpretive and hermeneutic sense in order to honor "the complex fabric of intertextual relations" (24). I believe he is saying that not only do we need to address these kinds of curricular issues (and forms) in our lives with the kind of complexity they require/deserve, but that, in addition, we need to go even further by learning to "complexify" (Davis 1996, xvii) the acts of reading/writing/reading in ways that lead us to understand our own lives differently because of the relations we establish with texts. In other words, it is never just the text or the reader or the writer but the relations made possible by their coming together and apart.

This leads me in a somewhat tautological fashion back to my reasons for offering "A Traveller's Guide" in the first place as this chapter and, in turn, this book continue to unfold. I seek to demonstrate how my notion of complexifying the shared acts of reading and writing move both with and against some of the ways identified by Sumara. I am interested, for example, in the potentially rich and productive con/fusion that can result from the intentionally ambiguous naming of form(s).

In my own fumblings toward a middle way, for example, I seek a strategy that might allow me to introduce the particular text that follows, in a manner that Sumara has suggested, as "an object that announces the possibility for an interpretive location...a space opened up by the *relations* among reader, text, and the contexts of reading" (Sumara 1995, 20). My intentions are (toward) complex(ity), however, in that I wish to culturally announce this text as literary—as poetry and fiction, but *also* as pedagogical and scholarly—as poetry and nonfiction and educational research. Again, my intentions are not to confuse, though they have intentionally confounding elements. In keeping with Daignault's use of "zones" as ways to move with/in the gaps and spaces of our textual living and dwelling, Linda Hutcheon (1992) suggests that this kind of (confounding) experimentation with text occurs in a place and space she calls "the interzone"...the space between forms and genres: between poetry and prose...between critical essay and ironic story...between biography and fiction...between performance and writing (13). Perhaps the interzone is, in this way, a part of the in-between, the beginnings of a middle way—a way for educational researchers interested in the generative (and generous) potential of ambiguous textual locations that become available through interpretive work.

Hermeneutically conceived, then, my sense of textual, tautological vertigo is always and already an un/familiar feeling with un/familiarity as I choose to spend time in "the interzone," where even the most "careful attending to the details of experience [can lead to] a foolhardiness of saying too early what the world is like" (Smith 1994, 16). "A Bowl of Yellow Flowers Stains the Canvas" is thus a "story" that is telling to my own research story. My aim in this particular exploration is not to employ experimental writing because it might make for a better story, but rather because the story I would like to "tell" aspires to a "persistent questioning of our taken-for-granted modes" (Davis 1996, 26) of telling stories. Further, I believe there is curricular value in dwelling with texts that have the potential to resist our namings either by "formal experiment or self-conscious play with language and conventions" (Hutcheon 1992, 14). It is in these kinds of ways that I see the "interzone" as part of a tangle—a curricularly fecund and generous place to spend time as part of a life that includes the practice of reading and writing.

And so, finally, I offer an invitation in/to story; "Whether you see it as arch or honest, as irritating or entertaining...its concern for itself as text, as language is hard to ignore" (Hutcheon 1992, 11). My intention is "to tell stories that end in neither comprehended knowledge nor in incapacitating textual undecidability" (Spanos, in Lather 1991, 151). Aspiring to the tradition that Sumara (1996b) has termed "hermeneutic postmodern pedagogical practices...ones which create curricular forms that serve to rearrange perceptions of the familiar" (45), the hopes I hold for the journey to come are earnest hopes. Returning to Cixous:

> The thing that is both known and unknown, the most unknown and the best unknown, this is what we are looking for when we write. We go toward the best known unknown thing, where knowing and not knowing touch, where we hope we will know what is unknown. Where we hope we will not be afraid of understanding the incomprehensible, facing the invisible, hearing the inaudible, thinking the unthinkable, which is of course: thinking. Thinking is trying to think the unthinkable: thinking the thinkable is not worth the effort. (1993, 38)

My hopes are also playful hopes, as exemplified by "fiction" writer Douglas Glover in *Likely Stories: A Postmodern Sampler* (1992):

> Note. Already this is not the story I wanted to tell. That is buried, gone, lost . . . I am trying to give you the truth, though I could try harder, and only refrain because I know that that way leads to madness. So I offer an approximation, a shadow play, such as would excite children, full of blind spots and irrelevant adumbrations, too little in parts; elsewhere too much. Alternately I will frustrate you and lead you astray. I can only say that, at the outset, my intention was otherwise; I sought only clarity and simple conclusions. Now I know the worst—that reasons are out of joint with actions, that my best explanation will be obscure, subtle, and unsatisfying, and the human mind is a tangle of unexplored pathways. (112)

This is my hope-full intention, my strategic desire: to move forward with words, one word at a time, full of blind spots and irrelevant adumbrations, so that together we might be/come lost and found, blindly with words...

This is where you are now. Then you turn your head away and you
are somewhere else. The only truth is that there is none: it moves when
we blink.

(Already) (There Is) Something About This Wall: An Unfolding...

Truth is made rather than found (Rorty, in Sumara 1996a, 119).

Here is a broad stone wall flicking alive small green flames of lizards. The
wall is low: I sit on its back watching the road that curves around the
wet blue belly of the sea.

Already there is something about this wall, something about
this orderly collection of stone that demands patience and
curiosity. I cannot yet say what this something is, though I am
compelled to wait here for some kind of unfolding. Maybe it is
only the promise of a story that holds me in place, a deliberate
building with words—word upon word upon word—that makes
the road worth watching; this *road that curves around the wet blue*
belly of the sea.

The sea is always itself, restless, forever altering its colours like a sad
eye; the road itself never shifts; the squat wall I balance on is like the
tough arm of an old fisherman. It keeps children and old women from
dancing off the cliffs.

Yes, I am sure now about the wall. The wall is why I have
come. I know little else. So I will practice. Practice watching,
practice waiting. I will try to pay attention. I will begin to notice
everything about the wall. I will begin to believe in the wall. At
the same time, I will begin to see that the wall is unbelievable. I
will begin to build a wall of my own; I will also begin to tear it
down. *The road itself never shifts.* I will begin to see that the wall is a
story and that the story is *the tough arm of an old fisherman.* I will
begin to see that the wall announces a location, one that makes all
the colors of the ocean possible. I will begin to see from the wall
that the boundaries between sea and sky are illusory. I will begin
to see that the wall is a theory, and that theory is a story that *keeps*
children and old women from dancing off the cliffs. And in case I get
lost, I will think of practice as "a pragmatic entryway into a

theoretical (analytical) problematics...[that] should be approached with caution" (Felman 1987, 5).

I am not certain about old women, but I have heard that children make the best theorists, "since they have not yet been educated into accepting our routine social practices as 'natural,' and so insist on posing to those practices the most embarrassingly general and fundamental questions, regarding them with a wondering estrangement which we adults have long forgotten" (Eagleton, in hooks 1994, 59). We are, of course, (most) familiar with the singsong-voiced chorus of children trying on the alphabet for size, embracing with a frighten/ed/ing innocence—the adult symbols of an (other) worldly discourse, symbols that, for now, masquerade as colorful building blocks that can be stacked and put away behind the activity center in preparation for afternoon rest period. Perhaps we are not as accustomed to listening to voices that begin to resist the chorus, the notes that ring hollow and already begin to form silent songs of protest. As David Levin (cited in Davis 1996) listens to Gilles Deleuze: "If the protests of children were heard in kindergarten, if their questions were attended to, it would be enough to explode the entire educational system" (275). Maybe they are questions that have to do with walls: What *is* a wall? Why is the wall (here)? What is the wall made of? What's on the other side of the wall? Can I climb the wall? What does it look like from the top of the wall? The bottom? Does the wall have a name? Can I give the wall a name? Can I see the wall? Touch the wall? Wall? What wall?

I am not surprised that we try to keep children and old women from dancing off cliffs. Perhaps we do so with our own safety in mind. I am also not surprised that, if we let ourselves, dancing would be the method-of-choice for such an event, filled as it is with such risk and excitement. Walls beg questions which are not followed easily by answers. How might a life that includes writing help to rewrite a life that includes learning and teaching? Perhaps children (and other spirited re-searchers) bring us valuable new ways to look at walls. And so, the dance.

I am not a child so my questions—these questions that insist on presenting themselves with unpredictable regularity—try to turn the wall into something other than a wall, into something

other. My vision is metaphorical. My imagination leads to a
pedagogical place and space far from *the road itself* where theory
and practice make a "paradise of words" possible (Barthes 1975,
8). For it seems to me that
a wall
in theory
is a good place
for practice—a good place
for *writing* practice,
a good place for
writing research,
for writing theory into practice into
theoryintopracticeintotheory—
for writing, for researching   for
being written, for
playing and working with words
even though words can also be
a wall.

It seems to me that "we must continually claim theory as [a]
necessary [form of] practice" (hooks 1994, 69) as we go about
trying to (re)imagine what research is. It is not a matter of saying
that theory is theory, and practice is practice, and metaphor is
metaphor. Similarly, we cannot point to a wall and say that the
wall is a wall. Theory is metaphor that comes in all shapes and
sizes. Practice, along with its own perverse set of metaphors, is the
result of our theorizing, our writing and building the world as we
imagine it.

The wall and the world are, in this way, interchangeable parts
of a sentence: The wall makes the world possible. Or, perhaps the
wall *is* the world, or our way of watching the world, positioning
the world, being positioned by it. We might build our theory
based on our practice of building the wall, just as we might build
our practice out of our theory of the wall, often one stone at a
time. Often we have little idea of the kind of task we are taking on,
little idea of what we are getting into, yet we do it all the same.
Witness John Jerome, author of *Stone Work: Reflections on Serious
Play and Other Aspects of Country Life*, who, in an odd way, belongs

with Connelly's sun-glazed images of an exotic and restless sea as he ponders stone walls in rural New England.

> A decade later I was seized again by the idea of similar, almost purposeless, wall-building. It was just about the dumbest piece of work I could conceive, and I took it on grinning, amused at my own perversity, full of fantasies about stone walls leading off in all directions, stringing these hills and fields together, organizing the world. (Jerome 1989, 7)

Whether it is the world, a poem, a curriculum, or a canvas, we "envision the hole in the air that the wall makes, then fill it" (Jerome 1989, 7). The wall, then, like a poem or a canvas or curriculum, "is meant to direct attention, to provoke response, to rearrange the familiar so that it is understood differently...it presents possibilities" (Sumara and Davis 1996, 2). In this way, the wall within this story—the wall within a wall—becomes a commonplace location.

Here we are, los domingueros, the Sunday people, drunk to exhaustion with light and the dusty scent of African wind. The bright blue benches behind me are soft with the bodies of old people, tense with the knuckles and knees of young lovers. The old people wait patiently for the farther darkness, the young for the closer one. They sigh anxiously, almost painfully, glancing in happy anguish at each other's fingers and chins.

This story is not mine. I would like to tell you otherwise. I would like to claim the light and the *dusty scent of African wind.* I cannot. The words blow in on the trade winds with an invitation to follow. In theory, they could be mine. The text, the story—*this squat wall I balance on*—is "the place where the death of language is glimpsed" (Barthes 1975, 6).

It's so easy to lose our balance *drunk to exhaustion with light* and language. Author-ity is easily misplaced as we write and as we are written. The wall is a wonderfully dangerous place to be under such circumstances. In lucid moments, we remember that the story is just a story. The wet blue belly of the sea is artifice that helps us suspend our disbelief. In turn, the wall causes us to question our beliefs, it reminds us that our beliefs are simply another kind of story, another kind of theory, another storied theory, another theoried story.

If you sit on a bench, the wall cuts the landscape in half: you cannot see the road below or the little restaurant on the beach where black guard-dogs sit on the roof, glaring at customers. From a bench, the landscape is picturesque: you receive the sea rising up like a mirror to the sky, slow ships sweeping the harbour like women in evening gowns, the grand old mansions reigning the far cliffs.

If you sit on the wall (but no one else does, for sun, olives, and wind unbalance, and the drop would be lethal), you get a wider angle. The back-arch of the waves stretches toward you, warm as a cat begging hands. There is something about the sea that makes you want to reach out…Below, the beach is speckled with people, scurrying with energetic crabs and children and dogs. The dogs are bounding through the sand, barking, pleading with stones to come alive and throw themselves into the air. The dogs see, blissfully, with their noses. They are enthusiastic about dead squid. From here, it looks clean, children tumbling playfully, doll-limbed, the people (featureless, really, at this distance) fine and strong, leaving well-formed footprints behind them. But you also recall occasional smudges of tar, the condom-scatter of spent Catholic boys on Saturday mornings, the shredded glitter of dead fish. Still, from the wall, the scene gleams, glassed-over, lovely.

Here, amid metaphors of theory and practice and walls
that stretch out before the sea,
I believe I am changing
my feelings
of how it might be to go
dancing off   cliffs. I am choosing
the in-between
place—the place between the farther
darkness and the closer
one.   *The back-arch of the waves stretches toward you,*
warm
as a cat begging
hands…

Hermeneutics and a Broad Stone Wall:
A Generous Location for Interpretation

Who can catch the invisible, sing the unnameable though soul snatched
up and spun through cupola and mosaic, turn wax. (Cook, in Castlebury, 1995)

In an oft-quoted passage, Madeleine Grumet has said "that to be
an artist is to perpetually negotiate the boundary that separates
aesthetic from mundane experience" (1988, 79). The stone wall
that offers us the view of the road and the sea is, in many ways,
this boundary made visible. How many of us, for example, notice
we are even sitting on the wall until we are invited to experience it
as a *broad stone wall flicking alive small green flames of lizards?* Is it
still the same wall? Is the sea that changes color a result of our
observing it or simply making it so? For me, poetry is (like) the
wall. From the mundane—sitting on a broad stone wall—and very
concrete particulars of our lives, emerge the possible forms for our
living and writing. The world blooms. For me, poetry is like
pedagogy. The boundary is shifting and negotiable, "a place
where meaning unfolds. The act of building, then, occurs through
a process of dwelling and, at the same time, for the purposes of
dwelling" (Sumara 1996a, 160). And, pedagogy is like poetry. Our
learning falls out in ways that never fail to surprise. Words are
small comforts that anchor us like balloons. We can only marvel at
the weightlessness of all that color. Poetry and pedagogy...
    The wall becomes a (curricular) form that "serve[s] to
rearrange [our] perceptions of the familiar" (Sumara 1996b, 45),
yet it is not so much the wall, or the road, or the *beach...speckled
with people, scurrying with energetic crabs and children and dogs.* As
Sumara and Davis (1996) remind us, "it is not in the 'things
themselves' but, rather, in the relational space between and
among particular objects, artifacts, and events" (2). So, the broad
stone wall and the text in which it is embedded—and the "story"
it makes possible—become a "'commonplace location' for hermeneutic interpretation" (Sumara 1996b). That is, all of our
writing and living and teaching—and our researching of all of
these—comes from the middle of a highly complex, highly
intertextual web of relations: a kind of tangle. "To engage in
hermeneutics—to interpret—then, is to tug at the threads of this

existential text, realizing that, in tugging, the texture of the entire fabric is altered" (Davis 1996, 20).

My teaching and learning and writing and research are all part of the wall. My writing life and my interest in the writing lives of a group of preservice teachers is inextricably woven in with the wall and the waves, but it will take time to tell the story. For now, I offer a series of textual interjections I call "Small Imaginings"—small slices of research wonderings that have been made possible by Karen Connelly's generous commonplace location. I introduce these imaginings, not simply to add yet another font that might draw attention to itself and add complexity to the form, but because they are always and already part of the complexity of this hermeneutic endeavor. Such a task requires that I work, as Roland Barthes has suggested, like a "Chinese shadow-caster who simultaneously shows his audience both the positioning of his hands and the silhouette of the duck or the wolf or rabbit as they cast upon the wall"(Barthes, in Harris, 1987, 160).

> ...Imagine a space. A soon-to-become-place.[10] A location. A (writing-styled) work-shop. Imagine that a group of forty or so teacher candidates, soon-to-be teachers, those-who-would-teach, live in this place. Let's say they're prospective secondary school teachers from across all subject disciplines: mathematics, history, technical studies, chemistry. Let's say they're wondering WHY in the world they're in a writing workshop to begin with. Let's say that, generally speaking, if you interviewed them before the workshop began, most

---

[10] In his book, *Private readings in public,* Dennis Sumara provides a valuable discussion on what it might mean to move from "a public space to a communal place" in a section entitled "Communal Commitment," 141–146.

would equate poetry and pedagogy with drinking and driving: a dangerous mix. Imagine, from the wall, choosing this as a place to begin to dwell, a place to begin to research...

"A Bowl of Yellow Flowers Stains the Canvas," and the world it makes possible, serves to raise questions about how we are made different by our participation in that world, by our reading and writing of the world and of ourselves, and by our being read and written by the wall and the world. *The wall is low: I sit on its back watching the road that curves around the wet blue belly of the sea*: "Something has been 'built' that has altered the way in which we understand our past, present and projected lived experiences. What words can be summoned to describe these experiences" (Sumara 1996a, 162).

Indeed, what words *can* be summoned to describe these experiences? What words will do? This is the generative dilemma upon which hermeneutic work—and I would argue poetry—spins: how to (sur)render (to) the world in all its (living) color and everydayness without reducing it to a lifeless portrait that closes down possibility. And: how to live well with "the knowledge that indecision, ambiguity, and tension are inevitable parts of living" (Davis 1996, 171). In most cases, there are few clues as to which strand we might be better served to tug upon and even fewer clues as to what might happen when we begin to tug.

Part of the complexity in addressing and entertaining a question like "What is the experience of living a life that includes the practice of writing?" arises when the question becomes a questioning that blurs the edges and categories of the questions themselves. How is each of our (writing) lives made different by participating in Connelly's text? Connelly writes her story. The teacher candidates write their stories. I write mine. *If you sit on a bench, the wall cuts the landscape in half: you cannot see the road below.* Many of my questions and concerns about the "text" of the teacher education course—the writing, the lives, the practice of teaching—are not unlike my questions and concerns over Connelly's text. Who is writing/reading/writing who?

And so the wall is a mixed blessing. In its generous provision of an interpretive location it also portends a certain amount of risk, *for sun, olives, and wind unbalance, and the drop would be lethal.* Still, *there is something about the sea that makes you want to reach out.* The wall and the sea provide an entry point for the beginnings of a journey—be it pedagogical or methodological, epistemological or poetical. Blindly with words...

...Imagine the class—that began as a mandatory language across the curriculum course—is now in full gear. It's mid-June. With four three-hour sessions per week for six solid weeks, and just two months to go until graduation, you'd think that the bodies—each now feeling more teacher-than-student—who share this space would be beginning to wilt. Let's say that they've been invited to work and play with words. To imagine. Their lives. Differently. Imagine that this invitation to write—personally, creatively, expressively—as a community of writers and educators is proving irresistible. Poetry is blooming in the most unexpected places. Let's say that writing is becoming a ritualized practice that is transforming the space of the classroom into a *place of communal dwelling.* Try to picture a kind of writing and living that would allow these classroom dwellers "to complicate their education and to live creatively within the contradictory world of teacher

education?" (Britzman et al. 1995, 2).
But let's say that you are
uncomfortable with the word
transformation and you are highly
(and not surprisingly) resistant to
these local stories of classroom
successes that begin to line up like
clouds on a predictable prairie
afternoon as they build into grand
narratives of perfect pedagogy that
eventually explode into shower.
And then they're gone. But, still,
you wonder. About this poetry. This
pedagogy. This notion of "living
poetically"...

"Could we say that our engagement with a poem collects our
personal and cultural experience in such a way that we are able to
engage in a deeper interpretation of ourselves and our relation to
the world" (Sumara 1995, 19)? From the wall, an offering of words
fall out in bits and pieces of poetry—*you receive the sea rising up like
a mirror to the sky, slow ships sweeping the harbour like women in
evening gowns.* The world opens out into all its relations as we
begin to develop then share a commitment—to observing,
listening, describing, wondering, interrogating—our own living,
our own wording of our worlds—pedagogically, poetically.

As a commonplace location, as a curricular form, the reading
and/or writing of poetry enables us to begin to theorize about
these relations, about our lives lived together, as teachers and
learners, painters, and writers. The poetic thrust of our work
together acts simultaneously to alert us both to the relative
inability of words to carry the true fullness of experience as well
as to the absolute richness of language and the almost inescapable
desire inherent in wordmaking which compels us to try to word
our own worlds anyway. *Drunk to exhaustion with light and
language.* It's easy to lose our balance. Everything approaches
poetry. Everything approaches pedagogy. Pedagogy and poetry.

...You continue to observe, participate, marvel at the ways in which a group of prospective teachers embrace language, become lost and found with/in language, revel in wordmaking. The students continue to take considerable risks with their writing and in their living and teaching; they build campfires with words, explode sentences into brilliant flashes of fireworks, dig holes in the backyard and bury the bones of favorite lines for safekeeping. There is much talk of teaching...

...The course instructor is a poet. He is, at times, a juggler, an accountant, an undertaker. A jester. A griever. A voice. A poem. A listener. Moving with language always, part entertainer, part interrogator, part witness. In myriad playful ways, the students take their lines and lives very seriously. These about-to-be-teachers—of physics and biology, English and geography—become poets of a sort, literally, meta-phorically. What is happening here?...

Our writing, even if it is writing we sometimes choose to name as poetry, is not simply about becoming poets. The "voice" that rings in the classroom needs to be not only "artistic and aimed at naming yourself [but also] political and focused on naming the world" (Lensmire 1994a, 10). Returning to Adrienne Rich's words from chapter 1, I am pointing here toward the experience of coming to live more poetically in the world where words provide "a way of thinking about poetry outside writing poems"—a way to "imagine other ways of navigating into our collective future" (Rich 1993, xiii).

Living poetically, as I continue to learn to embrace it, is living that is rich with imagination which, according to Gadamer, "naturally has a hermeneutical function and serves the sense for what is questionable" (1976, 12). Imagination, then, is not extracurricular, not some thing we use to achieve poetic ends. As John Dewey so wryly observed, "'imagination' shares with 'beauty' the doubtful honor of being the chief theme in esthetic writings of enthusiastic ignorance" (1934, 267). Instead, Dewey paints imagination as "the large and generous blending of interests at the point where the mind comes in contact with the world. When old and familiar things are made new in experience, there is imagination" (267).

For me, living poetically means embracing the hermeneutic imagination (Smith 1991); it is a living that is an inherently creative act which "seeks to illuminate the conditions that make particular interpretations possible and, further, to describe what conditions might alter our interpretations" (Sumara 1996a, 124).

...Let's say that you're extremely puzzled about what to do with this set of shared experiences you've had with this group of teachers. Let's say all the answers keep falling out as questions. You wonder if they're legitimate questions to be entertaining amid the scholarly traditions of the academy. Still, you are certain something important has happened here. So important that you're hesitant to put words to it. Others have. Some of them have made the words sing, even as the words are spelled as questions: How do we paint a "pedagogy of possibility... [in which]...hope is constituted in the need to imagine an alternative human world and to imagine it in a way that enables one to act in the present as if this alternative had already begun to emerge" (Simon 1992, 4). And: What kind of pedagogy allows us to proceed with some kind of certainty toward a future of teaching and learning that is "highly specific, contextual, perspectival, constructed, and in a sense, unrepeatable?" (Britzman et al. 1995, 5). And: What happens when we treat the liminal space indicated by the hyphen in 'student-teacher' as "a haunted and generative space, full of tales told to anyone who will listen?" (Jardine 1994b, 18)...

...OK, so you try a few of your own: What *is* a poet? What *is* poetry? How does the naming of someone, a poet or a teacher, shape and influence our relations with the named? How does the naming of an activity change the activity? change us? Other questions follow: What does becoming a poet have to do with becoming a teacher? What does becoming a teacher have to do with becoming a poet? What are the similarities/differences between a conversation that takes place in a café and a one that takes place in a classroom? What are the conditions that poets/writers create/require to "make poetry"? What might these conditions have to do with "making pedagogy"? Can we be "taught" to be/come teachers?

Can we be "taught" to be/come
poets? What are the conditions that
might help create an interpretive
location for addressing these kinds
of questions?...

Living and Writing and Researching:
The Moments and Movements of Everydayness

At this stage of inquiry, exuberance is more important than uniformity,
not to mention easier to achieve. And the conversations among
us...may need to be perhaps a little raucous, and to some degree
deliberately inconclusive, speculative, maddening, and pleasurable.
(Ostrom 1994, xxiii)

As teachers, writers, and researchers who work with others in a
world of wordmaking—students and learners all of us—clearly,
the conversations among those who have chosen to live our
classroom lives as questioning are anything but agreeable or
conclusive. This is the way things should be: *The sea is always itself,
restless, forever altering its colours like a sad eye.* If we believe what
we are told, the benches are a bright blue but everything else is
manifest through an agreed upon uncertainty. And then there is
the wall: obstructing the view, enhancing the view, privileging the
view, reconstructing the view, deconstructing the view, making
the view im/possible. We live and work and write and research
through the tangle.

The wall, borrowing from Wendell Berry's words, can be
understood "both as enablement and as constraint" (Berry 1983,
203). The wall is what brings old people and young lovers
together with the sand and the sea and the sky; it makes
positioning a necessity, causing some to settle in and others to
scramble on. The wall is not impenetrable. Worn smooth by wind
and made loose by rain and time, the wall is an opening—a portal
of possibility—an opportunity for discourse. As Leonard Cohen
suggests, "there is a crack in everything, it's how the light gets in"
(1993, 373).

Research may risk becoming another wall, another border that
keeps some things in, others out. Breaking walls down, then using

the pieces to build new walls. The task of sorting stones and moving them from one pile to another, however, is not the task that hermeneutics would choose to take on:

> It would be an exhausting business, almost a parody of human effort: tear down the old wall, haul it to a new site, stack it back up again stone by stone. Stone is another word for total: stone broke, stone cold, stone-deaf. Moving a wall would be stone *work*—hyper-work, Ur-work, mindless, brutalizing toil. Who would hire out for a task like that? (Jerome 1989, 6)

Although the hermeneutic journey I am choosing to take strives toward a thought-fullness, there is always the risk of demystifying, of poking holes, of squeezing the life out of those things I most care about. There is also the fear that I may not go into the places that most require my interrogation, attention, or care. The task is "both attractive and pleasantly terrifying" (Ostrom 1994, xx). And so it is that I proceed with a poet's 'I'—knowing that "the vibrancy and life of language is found in its living interdependencies, not in its lifeless fragments" (Jardine 1994a, 513). And so it is that I proceed with a re-searcher's eye with an aim, not to clarify or de-mystify, but to offer myself to the wall, to open myself up to the researching/writing/researching life, to engage in the "privileged act of naming" (hooks 1994, 62)—not for the purpose of setting up more walls, more restrictive boundaries—but for the purpose of honoring the paradox and difficulty that such a writing/researching/living requires. Through a poet's eye. Through a researcher's I...

> ...You think you are beginning to get your bearings. The classroom, this writing work-shop has re-verb-erated itself, become a kind of work-shopping, a kind of wordshopping, prospective teachers *trying on* both lines and lives, writing themselves in and out of context. Poetry and pedagogy are beginning to approach one another...

From the wall, we seek a "shift from the expected to the unexpected...the difference between learning *about* an experience or culture or event and learning *from* one's own reading [/writing] of an experience or culture or event" (Britzman and Pitt 1996, 119). We are beginning to think about "how to stage a pedagogy that is exploratory rather than content driven" (Britzman and Pitt 1996, 122).

But the view includes the road, which I watch in amazement. The thud bangs in my bones as I realize what I've seen. A child and a car have collided with the grace of birds; it was choreographed, her skipping down off the path and the black swoop of metal speeding around, catching her at the waist. Her scream is mistaken for a seagull's. There are thirty people behind me, oblivious as I watch a shadow dyeing the road (it does not even appear red—simply dark, like dirt spilling from a bowl of yellow flowers, her head).

There are shouts below, the single wail of a woman, but still no one around me hears this, no one leans over to look. I wonder if I am imagining all of it. I blink away sunlight and the cracked body remains down there, utterly still. The people around me (half-hearing the female cry) think only that the beat of the waves has changed.

As we dwell upon the wall, ponder our places as re-searchers, collisions are taking place all around us. To think that any one of these collisions might have the horrific impact that leaves dark shadows on a road is to make light of a child's life lost. Still, the immediacy of the impact, and the terrible intimacy of the scene the wall makes available, bring the writing and the researching, the writing and the living into sharp relief. Do the words, *like dirt spilling from a bowl of yellow flowers,* make death a possibility? Does writing/research enable us to express our shock or construct it? And, what kind of living makes writing (and researching) about dying possible? Sometimes, it's easier to *wonder if we are imagining it all.*

Although our pedagogy is not usually life and death, still there is the shadow. There is "something irremediably risk-laden, perplexing, and disorderly" (Jardine and Field 1992, 304) about any attempt to pull writing off the page "and out of the individual intellect into our sense-making, body-resonant selves" (Neilsen 1998, 174). The decision to embrace a pedagogy/research that goes beyond seeking technical solutions to technical problems—and which instead tends toward an opening up of the lives that we are busy living—brings risk and opportunity. As Sumara (1996a) notes,

> The agreement to allow disclosure and locations for interpretation during ritualistic events means that participants must understand that, at times, they will need to witness the unexpected, the unfamiliar, the tragic, the uncomfortable, that someone might announce (144).

...You begin to wonder about Michael, a history major in the class. Michael: a bit older than many of his peers, dominant and over-bearing in group work, his words and his poetry full of thinly disguised sexist remarks; the same Michael whose group wanted nothing better than to see him walk one thin line of his own prose, farther and farther, and farther still, until the words grew smaller and smaller and eventually could not support the weight of one so opinionated, leaving Michael to fall into a pit strung with his own barbed lines...

...And then there's Kendra, an English major: "OK. I'm just going to get this off my chest before I go insane. On my assignment, you gave me 17/20...I was hurt because even though my poetry may be only worth '17,' maybe you don't know how difficult it is for me to write and share it with someone. It just seems like I don't want to share it with you if you're going to put a mark on it, because it almost reinforces to me that I'm not much of a poet—at least not a 20/20 poet"...

> ...Do the quotes convince you? That
> Kendra lives and breathes (and
> cries) and, in fact, wonders whether
> she ever wants to write another
> word again. Ever. Do the quotes
> convince me? That I have done little
> more than write and rewrite Kendra
> and her 17/20 poetry—scribing her
> and then re-in-scribing her for the
> purposes of my own academic
> prose...

There is the *skipping down the path* and the *black swoop of metal.*
The writing and the living collide. *I watch in amazement.* We don't
often allow ourselves to hear the collision of the writing and the
living. *There are shouts below.* There is the *half-hearing,* but few are
those fortunate, or unfortunate, enough to feel the thud bang in
their bones as they "point the way with a pedagogical
epistemology to which [they're] committed" (Ostrom 1994, xi). *If
you sit on a bench, the wall cuts the landscape in half: you cannot see the
road below.* And what about the classroom—that real and imagined
space arch-welded into almost every individual psyche as a
universal—four walls that enable and constrain possibility. We
listen hard, try to pay attention to the moments that unfold, try to
capture the words that connect the lines and lives. But somehow
the writing seems to resist our writing (about it). The moment(s)
slip(s) away. Our lives are full of shadow and light and richness,
yet our pens often dry up under curricular or methodological (or
other forms of author-itarian) scrutiny. "[W]riting is always over
there in the novels on the shelves or discussed on class
blackboards and we are over here in our seats" (Goldberg 1990,
xv). *The wall cuts the landscape in half: you cannot see the road below...*
　　*The old people are gazing at the cliffs, ignoring the white threads of
cataracts, seeing perfectly the greenness of other lives, other decades,
thinking of the ancient lime trees towering beyond them—they were
smaller once. I hear serious talk about green beans and rose gardens, the
cost of carrots. The laughter of sparrows rings from the trees as always,
and the young men and women listen to it, imagining their hearts are*

birds. A girl with hair the colour of clean straw is staring at her watch,
desperate for time to slide open. Her hand flutters at the boy's silk-brown
arm and I can see what her fingers are thinking: There has never been
flesh this warm. Their hair is tangled and heavy with dropping light. The
sun rolls down the hill like bleeding fruit.

Despite the dark stain that gathers below, pedagogy demands
that we keep the conversation alive, stay with the living. "It is the
rupture—the break—that provides the interruption in our usual
patterns of living, forcing us to learn and perceive differently"
(Sumara 1996a, 156). "We are the bellringers. It is we who must
climb into the bell tower" (Livingston 1990, 216).

Blindly With Words:
Closing Notes on Ambiguity, Self-reflexivity, and Desire

A tune beyond us, yet ourselves...(Stevens, in Livingston, 1990, 13)

And on the road below (all I do is swivel three vertebrae in my neck) the
scene changes, a world bursts, the magic shadow spreads like a dark
angel stretching its wings under people's feet. The bowl of yellow flowers
is rust-red brown.

While above, in the little town, old women gossip, girls touch lipstick
lightly to their mouths, men grunt at the government, and I sit on the
wall, watching all of it, looking back and forth like someone at a stunning
tennis match, trembling (remembering all the world itself, the wars in
the back pages of atlases, whole countries spreading with shadow).

From the wall, I resonate with the words of writer John Jerome
who laments, "Words, I am beginning to think, are the specific
barrier against seeing things clearly...and, at the same time, the
only specific tool I have for penetrating the barrier. Perhaps this is
the writer's curse" (1989, 191). Perhaps this is also the researcher's
curse. We notice the light, the detail. We are moved, entertained,
shocked, perplexed, and compelled to wrestle with those things
we see and hear, touch and taste. We are choosing the in-between
place. Blindly with words. The wall disappears, though we lean
on it heavily.

...Al Purdy, a crusty old Canadian poet, would have told you in his self-effacing way that the poet is usually the "designated oddball" to his or her neighbors. David Smith (1994) reminds you of Wilhelm Dilthey's remark that, "feeling strange or alien is the first prerequisite to a life of inter-pretation" (Dithey, in Smith 1994, ii). You can't help making the connection between the poet and the researcher (you certainly seem to meet the criteria for both). The poet certainly lives a life of interpretation and the researcher often takes on the character of strangeness, oftentimes acting as the designated oddball. But then you begin to think that maybe there's a certain call, not to *be* different but to *see* different; it's the willingness to acknowledge the reciprocal relationship of ordinary and strange in living out the everydayness of our lives that makes us poets and re-searchers...

...Your questions are still questions: What are the conditions that poets/writers create/require to "make poetry"? What might these conditions have to do with "making pedagogy"? Can we be "taught" to be/come teachers? Can we be "taught" to be/come poets? What words might the poet and researcher have to offer one another? Can our treatment of these questions bear the possibility of remaining questions?

This is an interesting place to be: "catching life at its game of taking flight" (Caputo 1987, 1). The moment of inquiry mirrors the writing life itself; we dwell in those places where we are at a loss for meaning, those places where meaning breaks down. The tangle offers an ambivalent location for writing and researching; it is a place and space in/from which to learn to live well, a place in/from which to deal with the "loss of meaning by confronting the meaning of the loss...remaining open to the mystery and venturing into the flux" (Caputo 1987, 271). *And on the road below...the scene changes...*

This is where you are now. Then you turn your head away and you are somewhere else. The only truth is that there is none: it moves when we blink. The trick of seeing is not seeing everything. If you see everything and feel all you see, you unravel the wrinkles of your brain like a ball of kite string. You drift off and disappear. It is easier to be blind if the choice is between blindness and madness. Learn to see with one eye or both eyes half-closed. I look at the lovers, the lavender-haired old ladies. I look with great concern at my bony feet. Absurd tears there, gems of wet salt sliding toward my toes.

This is where you are now. Then you turn your head away and you are somewhere else. I am left pondering the in-between, the place between the farther darkness and the closer one. I am thinking about these bodies, these human beings who have often-times stumbled, other times straddled the awkward (liminal) space between student and teacher. I am thinking about old women and children, and wondering what it might be like to go dancing off cliffs.

Because, below, a child drains. The moment was a pebble-brained shark, and her life a bloody tear in time's soft belly. Now an ambulance clangs everyone awake, the people, even the lovers, crowd to see the crowd below, to glimpse the broken doll, the shadow. A shattered body collapses in my eyes, but I look beyond it. I examine the elegant web of veins on the backs of my hands. (You must look beyond.) I see the Bay of Biscay. I slide off the wall and walk towards a new place. The blood on the road will be gone at dawn and perhaps I'll forget I've written this.

...All that's left of the workshop and
the teachers who lived there are

echoes. Still, there is much listening
to be done. The (classroom) scene
has (un)folded. The teachers—they
are teachers now—have come and
gone. Their words and images still
remain, however, hovering; their
"meanings" refuse to crystalize into
discrete moments that can be
harvested, "nor [can] their
ambiguity be squeezed away".
(Davis 1996, 220)

*The wall is low: I sit on its back, watching the road that curves
around the wet blue belly of the sea.* This is what (the
writing/research) life is like. When you started out, there was
only the ocean. And, after all this time, there is only the ocean. But
now you have everyone's attention: *an ambulance clangs everyone
awake, the people, even the lovers crowd to see the crowd below.* You
have written them on to bright blue benches and beaches. Into
classrooms. On to walls. And *here is a broad stone wall...the road
itself never shifts.* And after all that has happened you realize that
"you do not know the road; you have committed your life to a
way, for words [*like dirt spilling from a bowl of yellow flowers*]
remind us of the past, demand the present; knowing, too, that a
certain awesome futurity...is the inescapable condition of word-
giving—as it is, in fact, of all speech—for we speak into no future
that we know" (Berry 1983, 200–201).

Already there is something about this wall; something about
this orderly collection of stone that demands patience and
curiosity. You cannot yet say what this something is, though you
are compelled to wait here, by the wet blue belly of the sea, for
some kind of unfolding.

*Here are the pastel hues (skylight, sea, warm green eyes, pearled
skin). And here are the dark oils. And here is your life. This is the only
canvas they'll sell you. Do not just paint what there is. (You'll be dust
before you've done that work.) Paint what you want to see.*

It's just like John Jerome describes it: "Envision the hole in the
air that the wall makes, then fill it." The writing, like our living,
like our research of the living and the writing is the in-between, "a

manifestation, I think, of the staring process, of all that time spent memorizing holes—trying to make vague shapes fit together in the mind" (Jerome 1989, 56).

> ...Imagine a space. A soon-to-become-place. A location. Imagine that a group of forty or so teacher candidates, soon-to-be teachers, those-who-would-teach, live in this place. Imagine, from the wall, choosing this as a place to begin to dwell, a place to begin to re-search...

Yes, you are sure now about the wall.
The wall is why you have come.
You know little
else.

the last e-mail

_____ an on-line
INTERLUDE

X-Nupop-Charset: English
Date: Saturday, 24 Sep 1994 21:07:29-0600 (CST)
From: "Geoff Sanderson" <sandersg@unixg.ubc.ca>
Sender: sandersg@pop.unixg.ubc.ca
Reply-To: sandersg@unixg.ubc.ca
To: rasberry@unixg.ubc.ca
Subject: Pretty Much Over...

I've been having some interference between "nupop" and my screen-saver which resulted in my screwing up the message I just typed. I presume that there is no-one left on the system anymore...

I meant to write a poem to send for the final class get-together, but the teaching has been keeping me very busy. It felt strange to leave Vancouver and UBC so quickly to take this job.

Gary—I've been meaning to ask you about your research for a while now. I presume it is focussed on some of the workings of our workshop experience and concepts that Carl talked about during the course. I am quite interested to hear where you are at in your work as I've been trying to bring some of the course ideas through in my teaching.

The idea of positive support is particularly important with the adults I am teaching as they have all failed at the high-school level so I need to do things differently. I can't press ahead in my lessons if someone is having difficulty because to leave them behind is to write them off once again. I have designed a term project worth 10 percent that is creative-based and open-ended and invitational for my math classes and have also been using a math journal.

Students are finding this quite different from what they are used to, and I hope it is working. The ENED 426 course outline contains a number of good references that I never had a chance to read and am trying to order them so I have some more ideas on how to use writing in the class.

I want to hear more about your research...
Geoff[11]

Printed for Gary William Rasberry <*rasberry@unixg.ubc.ca*>

---

[11] Preservice teachers are referred to by pseudonyms throughout this book.

CHAPTER THREE

A Life That Includes Writing

To write as if your life depended on it: to write across the chalkboard, putting up there in public words you have dredged, sieved up from dreams, from behind screen memories, out of silence—words you have dreaded and needed in order to know you exist.

—Adrienne Rich, *What Is Found There*, 1993.

In addition to being one of the most wonderfully long sentences I have ever encountered, the following passage is a manifesto-of-sorts for a life that includes the practice of writing, one that sets the stage for a group of preservice teachers writing across the curriculum.

I court conversation and perhaps consternation in my commitment to shake up and explode notions about writing, in my claim that writing cannot be conceptualized, schematized, and classified anymore than beachstones can be categorized and labelled, in my contention that idiosyncrasy and unpredictability and meaning-making characterize the writing experience, in my conviction that writing teachers must not reduce writing to lists of concepts and skills that can be taught to *all* students in ways that can be evaluated for purposes of report cards and promotion, in my devotion to interrogation and self-conscious rhetorical posturing and playful earnestness and contravening conventions, in my resolve to understand writing as the manipulation of language (material signifiers) in order to produce effects (emotional and ideational) in readers, my dedication to constructing a picture of reality that incorporates insights into chaos, the abyss, the flux, in my experience of writing as magnificently magical mystery, in my determination that circuitous, laboured writing full of obscurity and obfuscation (writing that twists, serpentine-like across the page and down the page, coiling back on itself, springing in a sudden frenzy of attack or slithering with calculated slowness) can manifest an energetic power by providing a site where the reader can dwell and play and dance in the production of multiple and complex meanings, in my perception that writing is not a steady, step-by-step progression through identifiable stages like moving a ship through the St. Lawrence Seaway, in my experience of the often uncontrollable aliveness of language, especially the relentless compulsion to write, listen to writing, to respond to writing with more writing, in my conception of writing as chaotic and risky and emotionally and physically demanding, of writing as exploration and struggling with words and discovery and growth. (Leggo 1992, 4)

The passage is written by the course instructor for ENED 426: Language Across the Curriculum, Section 989. The instructor is a poet, a writer, a teacher of writing. A teacher educator. His words, as this chapter begins, offer a textual location from which to consider writing pedagogy through a poet's I. And as I continue to read and re-read his words, taken from an essay titled "A Poet's Pensées: Writing and Schooling," I find myself replacing the word "writing" with the word "teaching" in order to observe how new possibilities are announced, how other relations become possible by the interchange of these two words:

> I court conversation and perhaps consternation in my commitment to shake up and explode notions about *teaching*, in my claim that *teaching* cannot be conceptualized, schematized, and classified anymore than beachstones can be categorized and labelled, in my contention that idiosyncrasy and unpredictability and meaning-making characterize the *teaching* experience...

I am discovering, in the midst of these relations, how writing pedagogy can become *writing* pedagogy. Through a teacher educator's I...

The writing and teaching continued to weave and interweave long after the "426 experience" was over, with Leggo's words of teaching and writing reverberating still. Geoff, a member of the class sent a "final" message to our 'on-line' group of teacher candidates from the course. The *last e-mail* is an important reminder for me that not only did the course actually take place, but that there were also possibilities for lives that included writing once the course was over. I say "final" message because Geoff and I did, in fact, continue to correspond during the year that followed the course, even though all that remained of our communal on-line group were the abandoned usernames of our colleagues, emptied shells, that sat hollow on the server. Geoff got a teaching job at a college in Prince Rupert, British Columbia, and continued to seek ways to bring language into his math courses. Sometime after that (final) message in which he spoke in hopeful terms about his teaching, Geoff wrote, "Well, I'm wondering about my experiment with 'the creative project' assignment...I got the first one handed in to me yesterday and I was quite disappointed. The student chose a minimal effort project just to get it out of the way. I hope this is not a sign of things to come." Our conversation had both of us re-membering Leggo's words...

> *...writing/teaching/writing cannot be*
> *conceptualized, schematized, and classified anymore*
> *than beachstones can be...*

Yes, idiosyncrasy and unpredictability and meaning-making certainly characterize the experience of writing and teaching. As Geoff's teaching life continued to unfold, so did his own writing. He continued to write a series of childhood poems, a project he had started in the course, in addition to writing poetry with his own students. A success story? Maybe. Geoff's words have partly captured, partly created a life that is "more real" for the poems he left behind. Lost lines from his playful poem "Random Thoughts" now echo whimsically of my researchings,

"...random thoughts fill
my head up
down in and out like
swallows picking up insects above
a pond. If you miss one on that dive, the thought is lost
and another fat one jumps out and says 'Eat Me':
Write it down quick..."

The rest of the teacher candidates, all teachers at this point, are no doubt writing their lives somewhere, too, but they seem as real to me now as the characters in Karen Connelly's "story." *This is where you are now. Then you turn your head away and you are somewhere else.* A bowl of yellow flowers stains the canvas. A group of teachers dissolve in solution with the world. The shadow-caster's workings are ever-present.

I continue to discover the importance, if not the necessity, of inquiring into the experience of a life that includes writing as though through a hologram. Seeking a language that might behave holo/grammatically—allowing me to invent words as needed and to observe lived experience alternately as the light and image gather to re-present new images that alter ever so slightly in the movement between writing and reading, teaching and learning...researching. This seems akin to Britzman and Pitt's (1996) notion of casting the time of research—the time of learning—backward and in order to necessarily complicate the practice of a life that includes the practice of writing. Writing research. *Writing* research. Writing pedagogy. *Writing* pedagogy...

* * *

"A Life That Includes Reading" is the title of the opening chapter of Dennis Sumara's book *Private Readings in Public* from which this chapter gets its name: "A life that includes writing." Reading-to-writing...writing-to-reading. What might the interchange of these two words mean to our lives lived in and out of classrooms?[1] The hyphenated space that connects the experience of reading and writing is both a generous and a generative space.

As Sumara points out, we cannot begin to understand the act of reading without inquiring into the relations that are made possible by our experience of reading and how this experience might "contribute to the ongoing project of understanding oneself and one's relations to others within the complex set of relations called the school curriculum" (1996a, 1). And so it is with writing which is, of course, one of the elements inextricably bound with reading in our curricular travels through school and, most important, through a life that includes learning (schooling and learning not always being born of the same breath, though Sumara helps us to imagine otherwise).

---

[1] Chapter 4 continues this interchange by presenting an interpretive reading of the experience of writing through a reading of Elizabeth Ellsworth's (1996) development of a "different kind of reading...a reading toward awareness" (138–139). I propose, in turn, a different kind of writing, a writing toward awareness as a result of my own "discovery," through the work of Ellsworth and others, that writing is a form of *reading ourselves*—just as reading is a form of writing ourselves.

Private Readings in Public (Sumara 1996a) is itself a hermeneutic rendering of what it might mean to bring our attention to those things for which we care deeply. Mary Aswell Doll (1995), another hermeneutic educator, researcher, and scholar, who also lives well with/in the literary imagination and breathes passion into her pedagogy, says that when we bring our (hermeneutic) attention to the work of teaching and learning, "Something Happens"…(42).

> Attention. A tension. A tending. These homonyms with their differing meanings residing within the same sound attract me, interest me about the teaching encounter. One gives attention to what one is interested in. There arises a tension between one and the material. The tension, once felt, turns into a tending of the material, much as one tends to the needs of one's garden or one's child. (Doll 1995, 128)

Sumara's work is, in this way, full of attention—a tension—a tending of the curricular relations that become manifest in one's attendings to the word. Throughout the many days and hours I spent with *Private Readings*—often in the beautiful spaces of Vancouver's new *public* library—there were numerous times when I became quite absorbed by the fine details of Sumara's attention, became caught up in the (at)tension of his work. I experienced my self be/com/ing obsessed with/in Sumara's obsession. Obsession, in this way, seems an irreducible aspect of hermeneutic inquiry as I have come to experience it in my own work as well as the work of so many others; at times it seems incapable of being brought into another condition or form. (As the preface noted with/out irony, obsession is always and already part of the body of this work.)

The experience of reading and writing brim with the possibility of/for obsession. My experience of living with a group of preservice teachers' writing lives became in many ways a shared obsession as we became caught up in word-making—together and alone. As Sumara, following Mary Catherine Bateson, notes, "deep learning often means becoming obsessed with a topic of inquiry. We [Sumara and Davis] have often wondered why these obsessive rituals are not permitted in school" (Sumara 1996a, 237). (At the same time, Sumara *does* note that any obsessions school life might entertain curricularly are usually tied up with "the real"—repetitive events that "suffocate the fantastical, the imaginative, the erotic, the not-present" [234].)

Obsession with "the real" and "the not-real" formed the backdrop for this particular group of preservice teachers who lived a relatively brief period of their lives together within the "fixity and flux"[2] of an extremely complex array of social, cultural and political forces at a particular place and time. Not unlike the experience of living in a very large city, these teachers-to-be lived out their days in ways that often left them feeling overcrowded and alone. In this case the group of preservice teachers, who lived in a particular section of a large multi-sectioned course within a large teacher education program within a large university (within a very large city), seemed well-schooled in obsession—at least with the hard-wired ways of schools, which often have little to do with teaching and learning.

Many, if not most, were often caught up in "the game of teacher education," caught up with "the real" as Sumara would have it. It can be very easy to lose sight of learning and teaching under these kinds of conditions, conditions in which obsession with "the real" becomes the "object" (within the larger game) of learning to teach. Learning becomes a learning to navigate the maze of logistics required to "survive" through the busyness—the business—of teacher education. Is it too simple, too trite, too cynical, to picture their living—our living—in such programs as a game in which the object becomes puzzling a series of colorful plastic preschool objects, ranging in size from big-to-small, one inside the other until only the large red container remains? There is an expression, the source of which I have forgotten, that says, "In life, we become what we pay attention to." So what *do* we choose to pay attention to?

---

[2] I have borrowed the expression "fixity and flux," from Jeanette Winterson, who says that "the emotional and psychic resonance of a particular people at a particular time is not a series of snapshots that can be stuck together to make a montage, it is a living, breathing, winding movement that flows out of the past and into the future while making its unique present. This fixity and flux is never clear until we are beyond it, into a further fixity and flux" (Winterson 1996, 40). I have held these words close over the time of the writing of this book. Polishing them and listening to them as poetry, as research, as part of a life that includes the practice of both.

Our course operated within a six-week intensive Spring session that saw preservice teachers attending at least two, and sometimes three courses per day, each class running for up to three hours. Sadly, this description will turn few heads. Worse, many will ask, "Well, what point are you trying to make?" My point, one that I will try not to belabour, is that obsession can easily become equated with busyness—hyperactivity—which can easily lead to exhaustion and the inability to pay attention, to attend to those things that require our attention in other kinds of ways—ways that don't necessarily involve the busyness of teacher education. Obsession, then, can easily become equated with the real. What becomes the real and what becomes the not-real?

Here, I do not wish to create an unhelpful dichotomy between the infamous and pejoratively labelled "busywork" of teacher education (and schools in general) and a more meditative and mindful work that might attend to the busy work of teaching and learning (though it certainly is tempting). Instead, I am more interested in asking questions about the ways that teaching and learning are about, and not about, obsession. In the midst of our busy lives, what does it mean to pay attention—to bring our attention—to our obsessions? What are the kinds of conditions that make obsession possible, impossible, bearable, unbearable?

I continue to be interested in the ways that this particular six-week lived experience in a writing workshop-styled language across the curriculum course (which was, by the way, not completely free of busywork) offered opportunities to entertain certain kinds of obsession through writing and rewriting the real and not-real, the present and not-present. I am interested in the ways that writing provides opportunities—creates conditions—that allow us to bring our attention to lived experience and, in turn, change—express and/or construct—our experience(s). I am interested in the ways that writing provides opportunities—creates conditions—to think about practice. Writing practice. What kinds of conditions are needed to create certain kinds of writing practice? Furthermore, what conditions are, in turn, created by our writing practice? What happens to these questions when we ask them to bear the additional weight of the practice of teaching?

Writing Pedagogy/*Writing* Pedagogy:
Re-Considering the Writing Workshop

> A class is a course embodied; it has a certain temporal, locational,
> dynamic, and personalized makeup. It has a specificity that cannot be
> duplicated no matter how many times the course is offered or taken, no
> matter how its story is told; it is a course caught in the act. (Crane, in
> Gallop, 1995, xiii)

Before discussing some of the writing and teaching and learning
that took place within the workshop walls, it is first necessary to
discuss some of the ways I have come to frame the ENED 426
class experience itself as a "writing workshop." In the following
section, I articulate the ways that my framing works both with
and against some of the historical curricular conceptualizations of
the writing workshop and the kind of writing pedagogy that has
paralleled/supported/created the workshop's development. This
discussion, then, is a reconsidering of the writing workshop,
where a re-considering is also a re-framing, a re-conceptualizing, a
re-visioning, a re-staging, a re-interpreting—a re-imagining.

In this case, the workshop, as a location—as a real and
imagined space—provides the potential for form and offers
pragmatic possibilities for talking about some of the conditions of
learning and teaching—to write, as well as to teach. In this way,
the framing of the ENED 426 classroom as a workshop provides a
location where preservice teachers could experiment with both
lines and lives in order not only to explore writing pedagogy
across subject disciplines but also to "raise thorny questions about
the inherited discourses of student teaching and to theorize the
contradictory realities that beckon and disturb those who live in
this field" (Britzman 1991, 2). The workshop, then, was not only
about writing practice and writing pedagogy, but also about
writing practice, *writing* pedagogy. *Writing* lives, *teaching* lives.

So the workshop became helpful as a location where learning
to write,[3] and "learning to teach, like teaching itself, is a time

---

[3] This chapter and, indeed, the book, both work to articulate "the shift" not only
from a "preoccupation" with learning to write to an "investment" in writing to
learn, but further, following Britzman and Pitt (1996), a shift to becoming curious
about (the conditions of) learning itself.

when desires are rehearsed, refashioned, and refused" (Britzman 1991, 220). The invitation for preservice teachers to write in certain kinds of ways—personally, creatively, and critically—was, by association, also an invitation to live and work and teach in these kinds of ways. In many ways, my intent has been to study a classroom "that offered opportunities for prospective teachers to transform their prior experiences of teaching, writing, and children as they began to assume the role of teacher" (Florio-Ruane and Lensmire 1990, 277).

For almost three decades now, teachers and researchers, too numerous to begin to list here, including Donald Graves (1983), Donald Murray (1985, 1990), and Lucy Calkins (1991) have focused on the writing workshop as an alternative to traditional writing instruction, as a learning environment that fosters "teaching and learning writing in ways that transformed typical classroom social relations and work" (Lensmire 1994b, 372). The results, well documented in other places, continue to play a significant part in the "historical and current drama of the struggle to redefine literacy in schools" (Apple, in Willinsky 1990, xiii). The writing workshop, along with a number of other reading and writing pedagogies including Whole Language, Language for Learning and Writing Across the Curriculum, Reader-Response Theory and Writing Process Movement, falls under what John Willinsky (1990) has termed "The New Literacy."

> The New Literacy consists of those strategies in the teaching of reading and writing which attempt to shift the control of literacy from the teacher to the student; literacy is promoted in such programs as a social process with language that can from the very beginning extend the students' range of meaning and connection. (Willinsky 1990, 8)

Since its inception, advocates of the writing workshop/writing process movement have emphasized "a commitment to taking students' experiences and meanings seriously...[an attempt to] humanize writing pedagogy through the acceptance and encouragement of student [voice] in the classroom" (Lensmire 1995, 4). As the workshop continues to find its way into teaching and learning, so it continues to be a source for both advocacy as well as critique. Timothy Lensmire (1994a, 1994b, 1995), in particular, offers an insightful reconceptualization of the writing workshop. He calls for a "revised, alternative conception of student voice—one that affirms both workshop and critical pedagogy commitments to student expression and participation, but also helps us see student voice as in-process and embedded, for better and worse, within the immediate social context of the classroom" (Lensmire 1995). He writes,

> For workshop advocates, the sounding of the voices of heteroglossia in the classroom is already a better world. Maybe so. For advocates of critical pedagogy, this heteroglossia may, unfortunately, sound too much like the already existing world, and be in need of criticism and revision. (1995, 8)

This discussion, then, serves a responsibility in honoring the many significant practical and theoretical concerns made possible by "The New Literacy"—connections to be acknowledged, forged, and fleshed out. Specifically, Willinsky's (1990) work "challenges advocates of New Literacy programs to explore new measures, to prove itself in difficult settings" (xviii). Therefore, before focusing on taking up this challenge (with the ENED 426 classroom as setting), I will first provide the larger historical sense in which "challenge"—as a way of demonstrating how the work of literacy, of language and learning in school—is always a re-working, so that my contributions are in no way a "New and Improved" Literacy but are offered, rather, in a spirit that contributes to an ongoing sense of re-newal.

It is my intention in this section of the book to establish a series of interconnected movements, first, between the Language Across the Curriculum and Writing Across the Curriculum programs (LAC and WAC) with/in and against a more "traditional-styled" writing pedagogy (as documented within The New Literacy), and, second, between one particular section (Leggo's ENED 426 class) with/in and against a large (and, in my view, rather unwieldy) multi-sectioned Language Across the Curriculum course offered within the Secondary Teacher Education program at the University of British Columbia. The discussion also moves with/in and against the larger LAC/WAC movement itself.

First, the LAC/WAC movements were originally established in ways that paralleled the writing workshop/writing process movement (thus, Willinsky's helpful and hopeful coining of *The New Literacy* as a useful umbrella term); such programs were intended to introduce "a radical program of studies along two dimensions, the one unsettling the school and the other disturbing the acquired habits of the student. This [was] to be a literacy which play[ed] *against* institutional authority and a literacy which work[ed] *within* the student" (Willinsky 1990, 22).

Reviewing the literature and perhaps more important, visiting the classroom, it becomes apparent that, in many ways, the results of the shift in literacy practices, particularly in the last decade, have begun to make a difference to the practice of writing and to the writing of practice. Those, like Lensmire, who have helped to carve out the many forms and faces of The New Literacy have seen the teaching of writing and composition move from its conceptualization as "essentially a neurotic activity," to a process central to self-discovery, understanding, creativity, and connection (Emig, in Maimon 1994, 14). We have made "remarkable progress," suggests Maimon (1994) in a playful but telling comment on the gains made by The New Literacy: "We no longer tell students that only some are visited by the Muse. We now teach them what to do while waiting for the Muse—and in case she never shows up at all" (18).

Current LAC/WAC and associated programs, while necessarily cautious in their claims, are optimistic about writing practice and pedagogy in schools. Students in classrooms are no longer empty vessels waiting to be filled up; "mistakes" are no longer considered "linguistic sins" (Maimon 1994, 16) but are, instead, important steps toward a more generous living and working with words. Still, in what is perhaps not so unexpected an irony, the LAC/WAC movement, in my view, has itself become somewhat calcified through a gradual reification of the many characteristics and attributes associated with language-centered pedagogy. I would argue, along with Lorri Neilsen (1998), that despite the significant gains that have been made, much of our teaching and research continues to be guided by "impossible metaphors [which] perpetuate the myth that literacy is something we think about and do, rather than something we live" (Neilsen 1998, 178).

The kinds of wordmaking that took place in this particular lived experience of ENED 426 created certain conditions for enabling a writing practice that invited teacher candidates to become curious about their own writing (and teaching) practice. In this way, as this chapter will illustrate, the workshop represents a kind of "metaphor of the possible" which "invite students and teachers into, rather than alienat[ing] them from themselves, their communities, and a sense of all that's possible" (Neilsen 1998, 176). All of this is to say that the workshop—one section of a large course—offered a way to begin to interrupt this calcification of language and literacy by offering a pedagogy that explicitly questioned and critiqued the movement of which it was a part—in the immediate sense of the multi-sectioned course in which it was housed, as well as in the larger sense of the language and writing across the curriculum movement (from which the over-arching ENED 426 course took its philosophical and pedagogical bearings).

In beginning to make this claim, however, it is important to acknowledge that WAC/LAC programs have now been in existence for almost thirty years, which allows me the privilege of being able to re-play history, to feel the weight of its existence, to take advantage of the benefit of time played out in patterns, and even to be so optimistic as to talk about what might be im/possible. In "Writing Across the Curriculum: History and Future," an essay in a recent collection of essays linked by their common concern for WAC programs (primarily in North American colleges and universities), Elaine Maimon states:

> The third decade of Writing Across the Curriculum is prompting many of us working in the field to ask the traditional question: *Quo vadis?* Whither goest thou? Where have we been and where are we going? (Maimon 1994, 12)

Within this historical movement—in search of patterns—I wish to show how, in the case of the multi-sectioned ENED 426 course, history has a way of stretching toward the future only to bend back on itself to show us to ourselves in ways that make the past only too clear. Said in a different way, history seems to repeat itself or, by way of cliché, *two steps forward, one step back.* For me, the irony is not lost on the fact that as far as we have come, we continue to drag the past with us as baggage for future travels. Still, my own work is made possible only as a result of this ongoing patterning of which I am part and privilege.

Running with the multi-sectioned LAC course meant enjoying many of the well-documented pedagogical "benefits" that result from placing language at the center of learning and intellectual activity: here was a place where the potential for writing was *real* and the connections were ours to make, all the while tugging on more traditional definitions of literacy and teaching and learning. Running against the LAC course was maybe not so much a running against, as a running in some new directions fuelled by a newly discovered desire for wordmaking, for celebrating the power of language and interrogating the practices in schools which enable or constrain language use. The ambitions for the writing project in the particular class of which I was part were, it seemed, less instrumental than that of the other sections—language was not only "across the curriculum" but also against the curriculum; it was used to tug *harder* on conventions and definitions of literacy and the living out of lives spent teaching and learning in school settings.

In the introductory section of the course textbook which was "required" reading for all students in the multisectioned course, Crowhurst (1994) states that "[a]s teachers, we need to be aware of language and how it works because language is the currency of the classroom...this book is about language, about learning, and about the interrelationships between the two" (2). This conceptualization of language by Crowhurst (1994) as "playing a central role in thinking, knowing and learning" (10) mirrors the LAC/WAC movement and served as a "unifying philosophy," for the workings of both the textbook and, in turn, the large number of students enrolled in the multi-sectioned course. Designed specifically as a textbook for course use, Crowhurst's book is predictably and, perhaps, necessarily broad in its presentation of language and learning across the curriculum. Sampling the Table of Contents, the first section, entitled "Language," contains the following chapters:

Language: Its Structure and Use
Language Acquisition, Language in the Classroom
The Language of Specific Disciplines

The second section, entitled "Strategies for Learning Through Language," contained the following chapters:
Reading in the Content Areas: Theoretical Issues
Strategies for Teaching Reading in Content Areas
Writing Processes: Theory and Pedagogy
Writing to Learn
Teaching Students From Other Cultures and Language Groups
Assessment and Evaluation

The text was presented as a kind of practical handbook for teachers, a utilitarian guide for those who have been prompted by the teacher education curriculum to look across the curriculum as a way of beginning to develop a theoretical/practical base from which to address issues of language use in schools and classrooms. In my view, the text, while useful for addressing the above kinds of concerns, does not provide any kind of assistance in placing the LAC movement into any kind of social or historical context. Instead, the text offers a rather prescriptive and apolitical view of language and learning and carries with it a certain obsequious "remedial connotation" (Lundy 1994, 71). One might argue that preservice teachers are already burdened with a plethora of difficult issues and simply need to be given a broad overview of language and learning, along with some "things that work" in the classroom. After observing the responses to the text (many teacher candidates found it to be "neat and tidy," flat and one-dimensional, in a world they knew to be full of bumps and curves and, for the most part, messy); it became apparent that the language of the textbook was not a living language; it was a language that was not curious about language.

So, the course textbook and its conceptualization of language across the curriculum, while providing a common source from which to draw on, also left room for a good deal of interpretation on the part of both students and instructors in the implementing of the course. As a poet, and teacher of writing, as one who lives with a deep and abiding commitment to language as a means for writing and being written by the world, the course instructor in our particular section (989) chose to emphasize a writing workshop-styled course—in my view, in order to entertain the bumps rather than smooth them out, and, in order to problematize and give shape to the discourse in which teachers find themselves being continuously shaped.

In "Transforming future teachers' ideas about writing instruction," Florio-Ruane and Lensmire state, "It is our responsibility and challenge to *initiate* prospective teachers...into the problems and possibilities of teaching the writing process inventively and meaningfully" (1990, 277). So it was in section 989, though I choose to italicize "initiate" in the above quote in order to draw attention to it and to suggest that, in the case of this particular course, "invite" might be a more suitable term. To "initiate" suggests an admittance to a membership or organization, which of course the teacher education program does at many levels. And while "invite" may simply carry the same connotation in a slightly different guise, I would like to suggest that the invitation to experiment with language, to play with words—to become curious about writing—was a significant element that provided the course with its particular flavor and sensibility. The quality of invitation made this particular section unique among other sections in the course. I suggest that this particular lived experience of ENED 426, section 989 created a certain kind of location that offered both the warmth of invitation as well as a call to be critical; an invitation that both welcomed and disrupted writing and writing pedagogy.

Throughout the course, preservice teachers wrote painful "literacy narratives" that spoke of a seemingly endless series of damaging experiences in schools. Through poetry and prose, talk and text, many spoke of the experience of being "wounded writers," growing up with writing in schools (Leggo and Rasberry 1995). As a result, teacher candidates often came to the writing situation with a good deal of insecurity and trepidation over their ability to work (and play) with words as they attempted to express and articulate themselves—their thoughts, feelings, and ideas; much of their insecurity, along with a related difficulty with various aspects of the writing process, seemed to stem from previous writing experiences in schools in which they were somehow "damaged" as prospective writers. As a result, subsequent attempts at writing pedagogy, it seemed to me—and the irony is not lost here—had to focus more on unlearning than on learning. It is significant to note, too, that desire was an element conspicuously absent in most of the accounts in which preservice teachers reflected on their own experiences of learning to write in school. Their literacy narratives seemed to portray a world of schooled people outside their bodies, outside themselves, unable to connect their ways of knowing to their horizon, their lives to their words (Neilsen 1998).

Again and again, the personal spilled out as political with "voice" becoming a contested term which, at the best of times, found a shaky fulcrum that offered a shifting balance between writing as both expression and construction—of self, of selves. In helpful terms, Lensmire speaks of "two related senses of voice: one artistic and aimed at naming yourself; the other political and focused on naming the world" (1994a, 10). This re-conceptualization of voice supports The New Literacy claim of being a "political as well as a pedagogical act" (Apple, in Willinsky 1990, x–xi) and parallels Britzman's (1991) conceptual-izations of the teaching relation as "dialogic," one that emphasizes "the ways teachers construct themselves as they are being constructed by others" (2).

Writing Practice/*Writing* Practice: "A Writing Toward Awareness"[4]

> The study of teachers' lives, whether described from narrative, postmodern, or critical perspectives, is beginning to inform our understanding about actual people doing messy work in classrooms (Neilsen 1998, 197).

The workshop itself did not necessarily change the conditions of the teacher education program but, rather, made good use of some of the inherent conditions already existing within the program itself as a starting place for writing practice. "Wildmind" writing, for example, an expressive, process-oriented style of "freewriting" that will be discussed at length in this chapter, became a particularly productive and interesting way to tap into

---

[4] This expression, taken from Elizabeth Ellsworth (1996), places "writing" in the place of "reading" (138–143).

the generalized hyperactivity of the teacher education program itself. (When not exhausted, the preservice teachers were often "wired" with and from the kind of living that accompanied their time in the program. One more coffee, a chocolate bar, lots of shallow breathing, a string of endless assignments due. Always needing to be pumped up for the next "event.") By using as its starting point this place of busyness, along with the acknowledgment of what Natalie Goldberg calls "monkey mind," wildmind writing became an apt choice as a workshop strategy for teacher candidates. Monkey mind is the busy mind, *that voice* that won't quit: the one that reminds us of ALL those ways in which we are inferior, interrupts us with minutiae, and generally maintains a flybuzz monologue that ranges from the inane to the insane. On any given day, many of us never got past monkey mind, never got past this kind of hyperwriting. Even so, wildmind writing enabled us, simply, to put pen on paper and bring our attention to the resulting words that spilled out in lines, straight and crooked. Sometimes the writing brought us closer to our selves as teachers—to our teaching selves, other times it led us further afield—helped us forget our selves as teachers.[5] And both were perfectly acceptable results. There was no "thing" to necessarily get past, only the satisfaction of being present in our own writing (process). How exhilarating this proved for so many of us.

It was interesting to note that critical questions about writing process, posed by the teacher candidates early in the workshop experience, and then later on by teacher educators and researchers reflecting on the experience of process writing, often arose out of a generalized concern for "where this kind of free-form writing might be headed." Writers, whether they were interested in directing their writing toward a poem, a short fictional piece, a history essay, or a comprehensive exam question, wanted to know *how* and *when* wildmind writing would get them to where they wanted to go. We needed constant reminders that wildmind writing is a technique only—one possible starting place for writing and composition that requires both patience and practice,

---

[5] Chapter 6 contains a more in-depth exploration of the notion of identity negotiation as both a forgetting and a re-membering.

as well as a certain amount of trust and faith. (See *working with wildmind 1* interlude for further discussion.) As it turns out, writing process techniques that include "wildmind" writing offer ways to get words on to the page which, in my view, represents one of the greatest stumbling blocks to writing of any kind. Once we begin to generate words, we can always shape them in ways of our choosing (more about this later). While writing process, as I am beginning to articulate it in this chapter, was only one aspect of the Language Across the Curriculum course, it is significant but not surprising to note, that it permeated everything we did together in the course. Writing theory and pedagogy—drew by far the most intense response from teacher candidates. Writing, and the teaching of writing, seemed to represent, for many, a highly charged, highly ambivalent issue; it was loved and feared in seemingly random and unpredictable ways.

Cynthia Chambers, a writer and teacher educator at the University of Lethbridge, in a conference paper titled "Composition and composure" (1996), stated, "There is a seven-character expression in Zen that reads *the instant you speak about a thing, you miss the mark.*"[6] Just as talking about Zen makes enlightenment more elusive, writing about writing dims the possibility of its true nature being revealed. I find strange comfort in being able to commiserate with Chambers, and her acknowledgment of the difficulties of writing about writing, in this case within the context of teacher education. Of course it is of little surprise that Chambers, despite the initial apprehension caused by her stumbling-upon-Zen, goes on to provide a piece of writing that offers excellent insight into the troubling aspects of the experience of writing about a life—about a living—that includes the practice of writing and teaching. It is also of little surprise, at least to my reading of her work, that "obsession" finds its way into her text, a text that is also her living.

> I write a great deal. Yet I am quite ambivalent about the practice...I find this ambivalence about writing as a practice and as a topic for writing

---

[6] I have quoted from a version of Cynthia Chambers's paper (1996) which was later published in *Alberta English* (1998). The italicized section within the Chambers citation comes from Grigg (1994). This quote is no longer contained in the published version of the essay.

erupting in my own words, spoken and written...words exist and they cannot be avoided any more than eating and sleeping; they are the tools of social life, yet within them is the possibility of discord and misunderstanding. Words have the power to create and change, as well as to suppress and hide...[yet] in the end, the power of words is what I have to understand who I am and how I can live well with others and on this earth. This is what I teach, or at least hope to. (1998, 21)

I am writing about a group of people who spent a great deal of time writing; this needs to be stated explicitly, no matter how obvious it may seem. This is in contrast to the amount of time we often spend writing (or in many cases, not writing) in our classrooms. Whether it is grade school or grad school, time spent writing does not generally correspond well to how much we know about the inextricable and invaluable role writing plays in our learning and in our living. Furthermore, the amount of time we *do* spend writing is often directed toward specific (task-oriented) curricular ends. Writing is, for many, a means to an end, a necessary but often painful experience.[7] I am able to book-end this paragraph, then, by saying that I am writing about a group of people who spent a great deal of time writing. Often with a new-found desire for writing. While the writing may not have been less painful, it was most often done in a spirit of curiosity in which the process itself was interrogated as well as celebrated.

The preservice teachers who gathered together in this particular classroom as the course began were not necessarily "writers." There were some who seemed to enjoy writing, while some were reticent, even fearful about writing. Others seemed entirely ambivalent about writing. The preservice teachers' feelings about writing and their corresponding writing practices could not be neatly charted according to their subject disciplines—neither before nor after the six-week experience. (And who would want to?) Stereotypes could not contain the many possibilities that characterized some of their writing predispositions and experiences: some English teachers felt

---

[7] It is at this point that, as a teacher and researcher, I feel compelled to provide a block quote in which I insert excerpts from any number of possible student reflections-on-writing to confirm my "writing-is-painful"statement. In fact, I will resist this research "strategy" in favor of a more writerly text that invites readers to write their own classroom scenarios into the imagined space.

terribly insecure and uncomfortable with writing (as did some geography and math teachers). Some biology teachers—along with some English, geography, and math teachers—embraced writing practice and became wildly enthusiastic in their wordmaking.[8] In the end the preservice teachers, who went their separate ways once the course finished, were (still) not necessarily writers. Instead, our time spent together, if anything, enabled us to explore and interrogate—to rewrite—what it might mean to be a "writer" as well as a teacher. (As an Honors B.Sc. undergraduate and an elementary and junior high school environmental education and science teacher, my own intense love for writing, which came only later in life, made me a perfect[ly biased] candidate for both suspicion and suspension of writing stereotypes.)

I wrestled continually with my own framing of the research experience, alternately embracing and resisting a Model (of writing) Pedagogy in which each and every teacher candidate might (free)write themselves into self-scripted sunsets where writing and teaching were bathed only in the most Romantic of hues. However, having acknowledged this bias, I can still say that a tremendous amount of writing (and teaching) occurred, much of it fuelled by a communally kindled desire and filled with an undeniable sense of purpose and excitement.

Throughout the workshop, we lived with words and in words, in part through a poet who lived through words, lived in words; he was a teacher who shared his words; listened to the words of others. He read aloud. We read aloud. With desire. Often. In a sense, we also "wrote aloud," where writing became a thinking

---

[8] My sense is that Language Across the Curriculum courses offered within the context of teacher education programs tend to "gather" around the "common-place" of language *in* teaching. Preservice teachers tend to become caught up in developing not only a "way of being" with language in their own classrooms, in their own subject disciplines, but also a language of experience for teaching itself, where language and teaching are inextricable. To live in language is to live in teaching. The term, "language across the curriculum," however, can give a false sense of language as some "thing" which must somehow be housed in different compartments across the curriculum. I believe, instead, that curriculum is housed in language. I have come to think in terms of language in and around the curriculum, language as curriculum, curriculum as language, where we are always and already in language.

out loud on paper. We began to experience the many ways in which we are our words, as well as the many ways in which we are not our words.

As I have tried to articulate elsewhere, with the help of Sumara and others, the practice of writing in the most literal sense creates a text—a location or place for us to bring our attention, curricular and otherwise. Some have said that writing is thinking on paper, or thinking-made-visible. In this way, writing enables us to work with and interpret texts that are "us and not-us"—"linguistic placeholders," as Sumara (1995) has described them: "Learning about things that we identify as 'not-us' means learning about ourselves. Learning about ourselves means learning about not-us" (Sumara 1995, 22).[9] Acts of writing as we embraced them in the workshop, whether they were directed toward writing an essay or a poem, or were more spontaneous freewritings, were undertaken in a self-reflexive spirit of both interrogation and celebration. These acts enabled us to engage in both personal and collective interpretations of our textual dwelling together. Paradoxically, we often chose to embrace our acts of writing in order to let them go, becoming self-conscious about our words in a spirit of self-forgetfulness.

It seemed, then, that the best way to begin to explore the kinds of conditions that made certain kinds of writing practice possible was "simply" to begin writing. In order to explore the kinds of conditions that made certain kinds of textual dwelling together possible, we needed text. To simply begin writing, however, proved to be somewhat of a stumble-point. The group of us who came to class every day, deeply immersed in a textual kind of living, surrounded by words always, found ourselves sometimes stumbling over our own words. Many of us were caught up in early anticipation with the possibilities of being in a course with an invitation to live in writerly ways. Excited. Nervous. Tentative. However, for many of us, when it came time to move pen against paper, the blank page—at least at first sight—seemed to be at once cavernous and restricting. This became, however, the hopeful

---

[9] There are several excellent sources in which to find Dennis Sumara's interpretive workings of the complex curricular acts of reading and writing (see References). For a detailed description of reading as a "focal practice," as well as "commonplace locations" in curriculum, see Sumara (1995).

tension that characterized much of our writing process, trying to imagine words where there were none before...

Within this tension—within the tangled location of the workshop—teacher candidates began to view writing practice as a curricular form that enabled possibilities for further writing practice. In particular, "wildmind" writing that included "wordmaking" and "wordplay," offered a for(u)m for *writing* practice. This practice enabled us, in part, to discover our selves, to see our selves thinking out loud on paper through words—even though words sometimes resisted our writing. The blank page: trying to imagine words where there were none before. The crowded page: trying to imagine words where there seems to be no room for more. Words.

"Wildmind" as Writing Practice for Preservice Teachers[10]

We are not the poem. (Goldberg 1986, 32)

As Bonnie Friedman, author of *Writing Past Dark* states, "We are afraid of writing, even those of us who love it" (1993, 15). Afraid. Of writing. Even those of us who love it. So where does that leave those of us who live in a place of fear and anxiety in our relationship with writing to begin with? In my experience, as a writer and teacher of writing, the single most difficult aspect of the writing process is putting words on to the page.[11] I most often begin with this acknowledgment—of the inherent difficulty and vulnerability involved in exposing our thoughts and feelings on paper. As a result, I often begin writing workshops with the following words from Natalie Goldberg pouring bravely from the

---

[10] The writing of the book has cried out often for the possibilities that hypertext might offer: "click here" to explore a particular poem or have a certain theory fleshed out in greater detail thus providing ways for readers to move more fluidly throughout the body of the text and, in turn, create their own pathways of meaning. All this to say, I have chosen to include a further detailing of Goldberg's wildmind writing in the Interludes that follow this chapter. I wish I could say, "Click here to go there."

[11] The "voice" in this particular section reflects the ways in which I also acted as an instructor during various parts of the course. As the details of the writing indicate, I offered a series of writing workshops that made use of Goldberg's wildmind writing theory and practice.

overhead projector onto the screen and into the classroom that awaits our wordmaking:

> Life is not orderly. No matter how we try to make life so, right in the middle of it we die, lose a leg, fall in love, drop a jar of applesauce. In summer, we work hard to make a tidy garden, bordered by pansies with rows or clumps of columbine, petunias, bleeding hearts. Then we find ourselves longing for the forest, where everything has the appearance of disorder; yet, we feel peaceful there…What writing practice, like Zen practice, does is bring you back to the natural state of mind, the wilderness of your mind where there are no refined rows of gladiolas. The mind is raw, full of energy, alive and hungry. It does not think in the way we were brought up to think—well-mannered, congenial. (1990, xiii)

There it is again: Zen practice. Even though I have held this quotation from Goldberg close to the heart of my writing and my teaching for a long while now, I still cannot claim to really know what it means. I love the sounds of the words, for the ways in which I think they might mean and for those ways in which I will never know what they mean. My life—my writing and my teaching—has been, and continues to be, made different by writing practice. Natalie Goldberg has offered me, and those I write with, beautiful words to write by, words that inspire more words, more practice. Goldberg's offerings of writing practice have created the possibility for us to gather around words, to celebrate and interrogate our words and our ways with words—for the ways they are like our experiences and for the ways they can never be like our experiences. Writing practice has helped me—and many who have joined me in the shared experience of writing together—to taste the fullness of words and know, too, the emptiness that words can sometimes bring. Isn't this like the experience of teaching? And living? Fullness and emptiness. Yes. I think so.

Funny. When I first began offering writing workshops *I didn't think too much* about Goldberg's words on Zen and writing practice. They became a kind of pedagogical talisman that streamed into the classroom on a beam of suspended light. I could point to them. Read them out loud. People would nod. Or smile. Or look away. Wildmind words seemed to be like a manufacturer's guarantee: I could stand behind them. Despite their insistence on demystifying certain aspects of the writing process, a process that has traditionally been written for us, Goldberg's words were still an authority I could defer to (in case they didn't work). Now, though, as I press for greater understanding, demand further articulation of writing process and pedagogy for myself, Goldberg's words are still just "words." I was then, as I am now, mostly interested in writing, interested in creating conditions that enabled groups of people to write together. Within the constraints of the classroom. Forty minute periods. Countless distractions. A certain demand to produce visible "results." These constraints are, of course, not surprising. I do not necessarily want to wish them away; they are inherent conditions of the place and space we have agreed to negotiate as curricular. This is one of the reasons I have gravitated more and more toward the writing process using methods like wildmind writing exercises.[12] They prove effective under certain kinds of conditions. They also create certain conditions which prove effective within certain kinds of constraints at the same time as they push out against those constraints. They point to the ways that we write as we are written. Not curricular victims but not necessarily in charge of the complex layerings of our curricular living. So I use wildmind writing exercises. I frame them within a workshop-styled pedagogy which sets writing into a certain context that must itself live within a greater curricular context. Writing. Within constraints. With possibility.

* * *

"Life is not orderly. No matter how we try to make life so" (Goldberg 1990, xiii). While I continue to find many of Goldberg's words truthful, I can still only point to them. I still know little about Zen practice. I am interested, fascinated even, by what I read about the practice of Zen but it is not my experience. Similarly, I don't know

---

[12] I should add that Goldberg just happens to be one person who has most recently popularized an aspect of the writing process/pedagogy that has been in existence for a long time. Virginia Woolf made reference to a type of free-form or free-style writing, while W. O. Mitchell spoke of "freefall writing." Peter Elbow (1981) also talks of freewriting with/in a more academic context. There are likely countless others who have helped to establish and continue to encourage this tradition and technique.

if I have ever met the "wilderness...the natural state of [my] mind" (xiii)—or anyone else's for that matter. I don't think I would want to necessarily. What *does* continue to interest me, though, is the following description that Natalie Goldberg provides about writing and, in particular, about writing practice and pedagogy.

> We can take a class from a writer but it is not enough. In class, we don't see how a writer organizes her day or dreams up writing ideas. We sit in class and learn what narrative is but we can't figure out how to do it. *A* does not lead to *B*. We can't make that kamikaze leap. So writing is always over there in the novels and we are over here in our seats. I know many people who are aching to be writers and have no idea how to begin. There is a great gap like an open wound. (Goldberg 1990, xv)

As I continue to think about the practice of writing, I become more and more interested in the practice of teaching. More and more interested in taking the word "writer" in Goldberg's poignant passage above and making it interchangeable with the word "teacher." It is this "close connection between writing and teaching" (Sumara 1996a, xiv)—and practice—that fascinates me. For the way I sometimes cannot separate them out: "We can take a class from a *teacher* but it is not enough"...For the ways I don't want to separate them: "We can sit in a class and learn what *teaching* is but we can't figure out how to do it...there is a great gap"...I stumble here over the subtitle I have given this particular section of writing: "Wildmind as Writing Practice for Preservice Teachers." And in this stumbling, discover a subtitle re-configured: "Wildmind as Teaching Practice for Preservice Writers." I will continue to talk about writing, but I will be prepared to blink hard when I reread my sentences wondering if I am reading teaching-into-writing. Reading writing-into teaching. Certainly the wall is low. *I sit on its back watching the road that curves around the wet blue belly of the sea.* The writing workshop is, indeed a generous location in which to take up questions, not only of writing and learning, but also of teaching. Knowing also that *"A does not lead to B. We can't make that kamikaze leap"*...

I am more comfortable now saying that the pedagogical practices of an instructor and a particular group of preservice teachers have created conditions that foster wordmaking—a personal, creative, expressive act that en-courages people to put words together, one-after-the-other in order[13] to begin to "word their worlds" (Leggo 1996, 233). As a pedagogical practice, wordmaking does not necessarily mean creating new words, though this is a possibility; it suggests, rather, the putting together of ordinary words in ways that often achieve extraordinary results. Sentences that surprise. Sentences that sometimes mean and sometimes don't mean. Sentences that unsettle. Sentences that offer places to experiment with lines and lives as we play and write and work at (the) practice and theory in/of teacher education. I will attempt to follow these lines and lives to a place of theorymaking in chapter 4 in order to find out more about what it might mean to sometimes know (and yet not know what we know) and then, follow them further, to chapter 6 to further explore teachers writing their lives.

Sumara (1996a), taking up Grumet's line, says that "following the line means taking up a life that includes reading" (9). Taking up Sumara's line, for me, means taking up a life that includes writing. Grumet and Sumara, as I interpret their work, are talking about how the world and the word bump into each other. Often and always. I believe they are both saying, in similar and different ways, that this experience, this bumping up against the word and the world can be both exhilarating and frightening, as well as potentially disturbing. All in one breath. The breath that follows the line: *meaning* the world with words. I would like to suggest that *following the line* speaks well to the workshop experience. Speaks well to the experience of teachers writing to learn. Writing to learn to teach. Further I would like to bring awareness to how fine the line is. Between teaching and learning. Between reading and writing. How the line disappears. And reappears. I would like to show how the experience of living a life that includes the practice of writing and teaching is an experience of following a line that does and does not exist. The line is real and not real. We read and write the line. We are read and written by the line.

---

[13] In fact, a central feature of wordmaking is that words that come one-after-the-other are not necessarily in order; this writing practice is described in detail in other parts of the book.

...Old thread, old line
of ink twisting out into the clearness
we call space
where are you leading me this time?(Atwood 1995, 72).

It fascinates and disturbs me that the preservice teachers I spend time writing and learning with are "being asked"—are choosing and not choosing—to follow the line while they are simultaneously asking others to follow the line. The line(s) lead(s) into and out of the classroom. Or, out of one classroom and into yet another. The classroom is an interpretive location. Yes. And, as Britzman et al. (1995) suggest, the site is "lived as anxiety...many experience the role of student teacher as an oxymoron: part student, part teacher, the student teacher is engaged in educating others *while* being educated...[which] positions the individual as both in need and in possession of knowledge" (9). The lines are tangled. And the lives. Lines and lives. Teaching and learning. And writing. Practice...

X-Nupop-Charset:English
Date: Tue, 21 June 1994 23:32:41 0800
From: "Tim Andrews" <andrewt@unixg.ubc.ca>
To: "ENED 426 talkback line" <brettle@unixg.ubc.ca>
Subject: Fitting 'Leggo' blocks together

Hi Everybody,
I can't help but be analytical about the way in which Carl's class works. It's my brain. For me, one of the largest factors can be summarized in a word: responsibility. In the university setting, Carl gives us the responsibility for our own learning by TRUSTING us to do the work when he sends us off to write each morning. He trusts we will do the work and learn from it. The trusting atmosphere plays a large part in the workings of the class, but often I am scared to give that much responsibility to a class of 32 rowdy grade 8's. Perhaps I am not trusting enough or else perhaps there is a middle ground where I can give some responsibility to students (as much as I think they can handle) without ending up with students walking all over their responsibilities. Just a thought.
Tim

X-Nupop-Charset:English
Date: Wed, 22 June 1994 11:06:16
From: rasberry@unixg.ubc.ca
To: "ENED 426 talkback line"
Subject: Fitting 'Leggo' blocks together

hi gang—

Yeah. Trust. Responsibility. I would add Courage to the list. I think Carl is really trying to live these things out in his teaching. (I thought he was quite funny and eloquent today in his "confessional" about marking and grading.)

We need to be courageous in our teaching,
gary

Following the line back to Sumara and Grumet's reading of it, I wish to reiterate, then, how the notion of "wording the world," as play-fully as I continue to interpret its meaning in the workshop context, is also filled with uncertainty. Risk. As Sumara, citing Grumet suggests, "the reader," and I would add, tangling their lines—the writer, the learner, and the teacher—"must relinquish the world in order to have the world...[must] follow the line across the page without knowing where it leads" (Grumet, in Sumara 1996a, 9).

Following the line then, as it snakes through this chapter: wildmind writing, as writing practice, provides for the possibility of a kind of "visibility factor" to our writing process; being able to "see" writing happen can be quite remarkable. (By learning to bypass our own internal editors, we sometimes glimpse deep insight into ourselves and our practice—of writing and living.)

One of the most impressive and helpful aspects of freewriting using playful techniques is how quickly a group of people are able to generate words, together and alone. Text(s) can be generated almost instantly. (I often use a writing exercise I have come to call

"Insta-Poetry"[14] which never fails to surprise with its results: short, pithy clusters of words that offer nuggets of crazywisdom.) The writing process-made-visible can provide glimpses into some of the ways each of us tends to approach learning, and in the case of preservice teachers, approach teaching, and ultimately, a life that includes the practice of both. As individuals writing within a collective we are again and again asked/invited/compelled to bear witness to our Selves—to our private inner worlds made public, if only to our Selves—sometimes for just the tiniest of moments. A window opens. A window closes. This is an intimate practice, but it doesn't necessarily have to always be this way; it is, after all, "only" writing practice. Wildmind writing, as an example of a kind of writing practice, opens certain possibilities for certain kinds of experiences but never is the goal to model a pedagogy that demands that the windows be opened or closed in a certain way. Neither is the intent to privilege certain views over others. Neither is the intention to have the window remain open—or closed for that matter. This particular writing practice, as a technique which may, at times, potentially transcend technique, is, in the end, a premise only. Try this. Give yourself to the writing. See if it works. Write fully for five minutes using this approach. See what happens. Follow the line. It's only a window. It's only a line. It's only five minutes. It may open a window to a life lived: the view provided might be personal, intimate, private. We might, in this way choose to see it as the window on the world—on *our* world. Or, we might also choose to see it as a window on a (possible) world—to a life invented/created; the view provided might also be playful, public.

* * *

Through a poet's I. I have tried to indicate in a number of different ways, how this particular experience of a group of teacher candidates writing across the curriculum, immersed in various acts of teaching and learning and writing, came to be

---

[14] Someone calls out a "topic" and a number of lines to be written on that topic, e.g., Epistemology (2): A big word for/knowing grown up(s). Or, Baseball (5): Hotdogs/soaring through the sky on opening/day like freshly hit/homers/(hold the mustard).

framed as a writing workshop. What I continue to discover are the ways it became a writing workshop because that is what we paid (most) attention to—to writing, to wordshopping, to work-shopping. I have shown the ways the workshop became a location, a place of possibility made possible by the relations between and among all those who lived the experience.

I have, of course, offered some of the ways that my own multiple roles of researcher, teacher, learner, writer, along with those of the course instructor, also a researcher, teacher, learner, writer helped to shape the experience. Passionate about writing, in love with writing, we both helped *write* the course into an experience that included the practice of writing. And living. And learning. And teaching. The teacher candidates were pulled by this passion, pulled by this open invitation to consider the profound nature of wordmaking, of writing practice, of *writing* practice. While the students were written, in part, by us, we were in turn, written by the students, by their passion for learning, for writing. All the while, the workshop, as a location, became something that was us, and not-us, of us, and not of us. So, while we wrote the workshop, we were, in turn written by it, through the relations made possible between and among the two of us and the teacher candidates (whose multiple roles also included those of researchers, teachers, learners, writers), and by our writings themselves and, of course, by the physical location itself that offered the cold comfort of desks and chairs (which we most often abandoned).

In short, we became
writers and learners and teachers writing
our selves as we were
written. Together
we re-imagined the place
of learning and teaching and writing as
a writing workshop   a place for writing
for teaching, for practicing teaching and
writing. A place for learning
to write a life
that included
the practice of writing

a life. In short, we became
what we paid attention to…

working with wildmind 1

I am particularly interested in the possibilities that Natalie Goldberg's work holds for teachers and writers and researchers involved in the everydayness of classroom life. *Writing Down the Bones: Freeing the Writer Within* (1986) and *Wild Mind: Living the Writer's Life* (1990) serve up pop culture and writing pedagogy alongside a steaming espresso and a side order of biscotti in ways that has the classroom feeling very much like a café. This classroom-café dichotomy can, of course, be problematic—the café may not be everyone's pedagogical cup of tea and debate over whether "Aged Sumatra" or "Arabian Mocha Java" promotes a higher degree of creativity may be considered not only politically incorrect but also atheoretical by many.

I must admit that my own willingness to express my feelings and opinions on Goldberg's work vary greatly depending on the particular context and audience in which I find myself. My Goldbergian proclamations range from evangelical accolades from the comfort of the classroom to sheepish, guarded optimism in scholarly circles. I am aware and often (overly?) sensitive to those in the academic community who would dismiss Natalie Goldberg's approach to the practice and pedagogy of writing as irreverent and unscholarly. Nonetheless, I have decided, finally that the café and the classroom might mutually inform one another in some interesting ways and so I press on here, as an advocate of Goldberg's philosophy of writing practice, and invite others to suspend various states of disbelief—if only temporarily—encouraged, in turn, by others like Wendy Bishop and Hans Ostrom (1994) who co-edited an important collection of essays titled *Colours of a Different Horse: Rethinking Creative Writing Theory and Pedagogy.*

Ostrom, a novelist, poet and professor of English at the University of Puget Sound supports me in my claim that thinking about writing pedagogy as being more café-like than classroom-driven is not, in fact, "a retreat from theory" but, rather, offers a way of connecting theory and pedagogy which "in itself suggests that students are worth the trouble—that to a certain extent, theorizing pedagogy honors the students and our profession" (Ostrom 1994, xxi).

This group that seeks to bring writing practice and theory to bear upon one another includes academics and scholars, innovative practitioners—"whose innovations emerge from the laboratory of their own experience" (Sarbo and Moxley 1994, 142)—poets and novelists, homespun literary hounds, and self-appointed writing experts and enthusiasts who operate writing groups based out of their own living rooms and kitchens.

This interlude, then, represents the beginnings only of an ongoing effort to investigate and interrogate the boundaries and intertextual spaces that have begun to give this pedagogical niche shape—a shape that finds classroom pedagogy more and more influenced by popular culture as both continue to embrace the writing life. As Donald Murray (1990) has suggested, "we need all forms of research and the testimony of those who produce the texts we read and respect" (xiv), whether the symposia take place in conference rooms or in kitchens. We can now read writers writing about other writers, about themselves, and about their craft. Annie Dillard's *Living by Fiction* (1982), and *The Writing Life* (1989), Donald Murray's *Shoptalk: Learning to Write with Writers* (1990), and Bonnie Friedman's *Writing Past Dark* (1993) each move beyond star-gazing pop culture to in-depth explorations of the writerly life and "how writing happens."

Theory and research into writing pedagogy has also burgeoned as writing has been given a life that lives and breathes beyond the classroom walls. In addition to "response theory," conferencing and workshopping (Murray 1985), "writing with power," freewriting, power of voice and "audience as focusing force" (Elbow 1981), epistemic writing and "plural I's" (Coles 1978), emerging writers are also being invited in greater numbers to bring their "wildminds" (Goldberg 1990) to class.

Goldberg's "rules for writing"—made to be broken—include: "keep your hand moving, lose control, be specific, don't think, don't worry about punctuation, spelling or grammar, and, you are free to write the worst junk in [North] America" (1990, 2–4). Writers are encouraged to apply these rules in timed-writing exercises. When used on a regular basis as writing practice, these writing sessions help provide ways to move beyond "monkey mind"—the tireless (and ruthless) editor who tends to rule most of our writing—toward a deeper, more generous and creative level of writing that has the ability to surprise the writer with unexpected insights and splashes of poetry in prose, whether one is working on a book, a research report, or composing a life.

At one level Goldberg creates an idealized, romantic version of living and teaching and talking about writing. (Is there anything more to it than finding a café of one's own, the perfect cappuccino and a PowerBook with a reliable battery pack?) At another level, I would suggest that Goldberg needs to be taken seriously by academics and do-it-yourselfers alike; her approach to living and writing offers much to all those who write, from the emerging neophyte to the seasoned veteran. In fact, many of these kinds of distinctions and polarizations that exist between beginner and expert are collapsed through Goldberg's "wildmind" practice and philosophy. There is the pen and the paper and the Selves that we bring to our writing, time and time again. Both the tenured and the tenuous must put pen to paper, fingers to keyboard, and place one word after the other in straight and crooked lines. We all connect the dots with words, waiting with apprehension and excitement, nervousness and composure to see what will come out the other side: our stories, our essays, our grant applications, our letters of resignation—of indignation and reservation, our poems, our earnest autobiographies, our lavish fictions, our diary entries, our books, our lavish autobiographies, our earnest fiction, our research reports, and our love letters to the world. In all of these forms and more, we bring some part of our hearts and minds to the business and pleasure of writing.

Wildmind writing, if we embrace it as Goldberg suggests we embrace it, becomes a belief, a way of being, a pledge, a craft, a commitment, a caring. Or, we can view wildmind writing simply as a premise: try this, give yourself to the words, see if it works. Then: try it again, give yourself to the words, see if it works. Wildmind demands that we let go of ourselves to find ourselves. Turn the spell check off, forget the word count, don't worry about what comes next. Goldberg reminds us again and again to let go of our "monkey minds" (mine sounding something like this):

> *I should be doing my income taxes. This sentence sucks. My committee will think this is absolute trash. I think this absolute trash. There must be a better way of describing the sounds of the forest. I always screw up under pressure. This thing is due tomorrow. I'll never be a writer. I'll never get my degree. I wonder what the score in the ball game is? I don't want to be here. I could be*

*board-sailing right now. I wish I could learn to spell apparent. Am I having fun
yet?*

Goldberg encourages us to work with our wildminds—the "wilderness of our mind[s] where there are no refined rows of gladiolas" (1990, xiii). You simply start with a blank page and begin to write:

> *Right now I'm staring hard at this TV blue screen, an academic artist whose
> coffee-stained words and cappuccino dreams of market stalls and strings of
> flowers take me in and out of my word-processed world while I attempt to meet
> this deadline and stay within a specified word count. Slumbering on a bed of
> semicolons now, rearranging rows of letters, I count the commas until I drop
> off or come to the end of a page.*

With Wildmind, there is no one way to write a proposal, no perfect place for a semicolon, no correct way to write a conclusion, no right way to write. Wildmind is rooted in practice. Wildmind *is* practice. Practice makes for more practice. Wildmind is unpractice. Wildmind is like walking, one foot in front of the other. We can always throw our writing away later, or perhaps chip and chop, shape and sculpt our blocks of words into different forms. We don't have to go into thesis-mode when the going gets tough. Our writing is there to surprise us, to catch us off guard when we're not looking. Our writing is there to teach us. The lessons are built-in. Wildmind is "writing down the bones" (Goldberg 1986, 4).

Of course, those who write and teach and research know all of this, right? There is nothing new here. Wildmind makes common sense. So, tell us something we don't know. Sorry. That's all there is. Keep your pen moving. Write. Then write some more. Follow your hunches. Write. Then write some more. Learn to write with passion. Learn (to ignore) the rules as you see fit. Does the writing have to be personal? Yes and no. We are not our words. We don't necessarily write to freeze our lives in an easy to view snapshot (like just another "Kodak Moment.") We also write to compose our lives, to make up li(n)es and li(v)es. We are not our latest poem or academic paper. We are not hardwired to our hard drives. We can always unplug.

I watch class after class trip and stumble on to their own wildminds: tentatively, reluctantly, anxiously, excitedly (and I stumble with them, stumbling after my own). My goal, however, is not to create a café/classroom dichotomy, nor is it to fashion an either/or-styled pedagogical discourse in which one is either using wildmind or pulling teeth. There are myriad stories to be (de)constructed about both café and classroom as places where our dreams for teaching and learning are both informed and contested. In the same way that caféd images of the writerly life slide easily into stereotype and become problematic, for example, so too, the classroom writing life. In a certain light, everyone might be considered "A Writer." Such well-intentioned pedagogy is simply not sustainable. There must be something more at work.

At the same time, writing pedagogy has come to a place where we must recognize and accept the notion that writing, like life (or life, like writing) is messy, unpredictable stuff. To live and write in the world is to live and write with "all the contradiction, paradox and living difficulty that such a world requires and invites" (Jardine 1994a, 513).

working with wildmind, too

_____ **INTERLUDE**

Writing #147a: [15]

Whenever I think of lime green...a dump truck rolls up and pours red bricks on the hot blue asphalt now one thing for certain is that the land the sea and the sky are just about glad to be issuing parking tickets to any and all soldiers because a war of words is better than no war at all and the trouble with gray is that mauve was invented and the light bulb's discovery pales in comparison falling into shadowless night after night green stars fly softly as if space were a garage door and never have I felt so awkward and ashamed at the sight of so much garbage drifting like swans toward the sea the surf belching burgers and every crazy employee you've ever had decided to show up in last night's dream and the sands move inching toward blue dawn stars attempt to reinvent themselves with Beethoven removing his socks...

Poem #1: Swans and soldiers

Stars attempt
to reinvent themselves,

flying softly, as if space were certain,
into the shadowless night—

so many gray soldiers, drifting like swans
toward the sea.

---

[15] We used timed writing exercises (see description of Goldberg's "rules for writing" in the interlude *Working with Wildmind 1*) as a regular part of each class and would then proceed to play with the words generated, sometimes working in small groups to chip and chop, shape and sculpt blocks of words into forms we chose to call poetry. The freewrites in this interlude are my own. (Teacher candidates, for the most part, freewrote in their journals and notebooks, which I did not collect as part of my gathering of data.) Note also that punctuation tends to be absent in the freewrite. The poems presented here were written by teacher candidates who took the words I generated during the freewrite and shaped them into forms that pleased them. The italicized words that begin the freewrite are a writing "prompt" that act as a springboard for diving into more words...

Poem #2: Certainty

One thing for certain:
the sea
the sky
a war
the stars
space
the night
I felt so   crazy.

Poem #3: Inching toward blue

The trouble with gray, the light
of the discovery.

Night after night: green
stars.

Never have I felt
so awkward

ashamed
drifting

inching toward
blue.

Free-write #147b:

*Lime green reminds me of...*blue shadows that creep across brown
rivers sliding sliding sliding toward red oceans hoping beyond
hope they might fill up with enough of life's liquid ok enough
baggage blah blah woof woof sometimes you feel three parts
whole two parts underwater again a constant theme—a liquid
metaphor that keeps my writing afloat when words run dry dryer
than any desert you could have crawled across during any
lifetime solo as the time beyond birth beyond what the sand might

offer faster still worlds bloom like desert flowers in a nighttime sky—a sea of golden brown as seen from a lime green balloon a window on some kind of world some kind of wonderful trip into another lifetime and time again you can only nail the words lightly upon the wall hoping another might pass by and wonder what the letters mean what symbols have fallen across the horizon of horizons bluer than blue should ever be green yet what color is enough to stop us all from ever naming the patterns that form behind our eyes, falling and falling as though this is all just a rehearsal and soon someone who knows the truth will raise their hand as if by some great and hidden cue.

Poem #1: Rehearsal

What symbols? have
fallen, blue.
What color is enough
to stop us
hoping?

As though this is all just
a rehearsal.
Falling and naming
the patterns behind
our eyes.

Poem #2: Symbols fallen

You can only nail the words
lightly upon the wall—
symbols fallen across the horizon
naming the patterns that form
behind our eyes.

When words run dry
dryer than any desert
words bloom like desert flowers
solo as the time beyond birth.

And soon someone who knows
the truth will rise
as if by some great
and hidden cue.

Freewrite #147c:

If gold were an ocean...I'd name gold blue and ask for a recount or
trade every one of my hockey cards in for a bigger bathtub or
maybe wash less often or count the times like tiny beads of sweat
that I have wished for the ocean to be my lover oh well every
good boy deserves flavor and salt water cappuccinos are a dime a
dozen just think of all the world's tides just think of the way the
lake fell away and no longer exists outside this building that no
longer exists outside just think about the time your cat flew across
the kitchen in some birdlike dream—a kitty mantra—a feline in
canary's clothing yellow or coal mine or death deaf as a fish is
some other like some government sometimes poetry can kiss your
cheek and all you feel is that the air has moved and changed
everything and nothing else matters and what if it did and the
more you eat the more you forget that poetry is breath is the
substance that makes you hungry and fills you full of summer
evenings and violin concertos in your finest eveningwear...

Poem #1: If gold

If gold were the ocean
I'd name gold blue:
Think of all the world's tides.
That poetry is breath.

In some birdlike dream
Of summer evenings
Wishing for the ocean—
My lover.

Poem #2: Sometimes poetry

Sometimes poetry
can kiss your cheek
and all that you feel
has moved and changed
and nothing else exists.
Less often I have wished for

the air and everything
as breath
your cheek
and nothing else
that poetry is.
Just think less

often.
Summer evenings and violin
concertos
and nothing else
can kiss your cheek.
Just think...

CHAPTER FOUR

Through the Tangle

Can a study of the self studying education create new conditions of learning and the making of pedagogical insight?

—Deborah Britzman and Alice Pitt, *Pedagogy and transference*, 1996.

The question posed by Deborah Britzman and Alice Pitt (1996) in the epigraph above startles me. Into awareness. A new(er) awareness of what it is I am doing, learning, writing, practicing, researching, in and through this book: *Can a study of the self, studying education create new conditions of learning and the making of insight?* The question shows myself to me in a way that enables me to participate in "the making of (an) insight": "Ah, I didn't know (I knew) this before." Until now. Didn't know (this is) what I was doing: attempting to enact a study of the self, studying education. Imagining the curious time of researching. Pedagogy.

As Elizabeth Ellsworth states in her self-reflexive wonderings about her own practice, of teaching and learning, writing and reading—of researching, "without consciously intending it or grasping it, I somehow 'knew'..."(1996, 142). From the beginnings of the writing of this book, which has no real beginning, I knew I was writing *about* the tangle. I knew that my experience of writing—about the experience of writing and researching lived experience—would be necessarily tangled since I also knew that the experience of writing and researching are themselves tangled. The writing of this research, then, has been an interesting trip through the tangle. An interesting trip. Through the tangle. Because it seems impossible. Not to trip. Through this particular tangle:

What is the experience of a self studying a self studying selves studying (them)selves studying education?

While I somehow knew the tangle, knew about the tangle, knew I wanted to "research" the (lived experience) of the tangle, I did not know what would be involved in learning to experience the tangle. I did not know how involving it would be learning to write the experience of the tangle, learning to experience the writing of the tangle, learning to experience the tangling of the writing. While I knew all of these things about the tangle, I did not know the tangle.

This chapter, then, represents an attempt to theorize the tangle through the tangled practice of theory, just as it is an attempt to practice the tangle through the tangled theory of practice. Theorypracticetheory. Practicetheorypractice. The tangle: yroehtecitcarpyroeht...

It is the experience of living a life that includes the practice of writing that has brought me to the tangle, helped to create a location through which to (continue to) write the tangle, as well as be written by it. So it is the practice of writing that I will continue to practice, continue to theorize. This chapter, as well as the final chapter, are both attempts to theorize writing practice—a practice that includes both wordmaking and wordplay. In so doing, both chapters (4 and 6) are also attempts to practice theory, attempts to practice theorizing by practicing writing practice.

It's easy to see, then, why this trip is through the tangle. Easy to see why it's difficult to move through the tangle without becoming tangled, since theorizing writing practice can only be accomplished through writing practice, which, itself, becomes a way of *writing* practice, which, itself, is a way of *writing* theory. So (writing) theory and (writing) practice are en-tangled and can only be practiced and theorized through the tangle.

The theorypracticetheory that I am enacting through *writing* theory and *writing* practice is made possible through wordplay which helps to create a (shifting) location through which one can continue to write theory and write practice. This chapter, as maddening as it has been to write (and likely will be to read), seeks to play with words as a way of theorizing and practicing the tangle through the tangle of wordplay in an attempt to enact wordplay and wordmaking as a writing practice which is (as I continue to discover) generative, pedagogical, curricular, relational, hermeneutic, psychoanalytic, interpretive, fecund, fictional, and poetic.

Through the tangle of practice, here is an attempt at (a) theory: writing practice, that includes wordplay and wordmaking, enables teacher candidates to begin to experience their own writing as a form of reading—a form of reading themselves. Further, writing practice creates conditions of learning to "read writing" as (a) practice which, in turn, enables teacher candidates to read themselves more generously (because it's "only" practice). In addition, it enables teacher candidates to read the writing of others—their own students, for example—as (a) practice which, in turn, offers a way of reading themselves as others, as well as reading others as themselves. Writing practice, then, which includes wordmaking and wordplay, enables teacher candidates to create their own particular forms of writing practice, of *writing* practice, which is itself a theory, a way of *writing* theory—a way of theorymaking.

So, although wordplay never appears to take itself seriously, it can, in fact, play a serious role in the work of writing practice and theory. And while wordplay tends to give itself a bad name and can end up becoming a caricature of itself, it can also help make pedagogy more than (just) a play *on* words; that is, it can create conditions that help *make* pedagogy. Or, in more scholarly terms, using Britzman and Pitt's formulation, I would suggest that writing practice can help create new conditions of learning and the making of pedagogical insight. Similarly, writing practice that includes wordplay can also create conditions that help make poetry more than (just) a play *with* words; that is, it can create conditions that help *make* poetry. Writing practice, then, can help create new conditions of learning and the making of pedagogical insight, which in turn helps make practice; this "making of practice" might then be considered a kind of poetics of practice.

Wordplay makes up words. Wordplay makes up its own rules. Wordplay can be a clever performance—a play that draws attention to itself. Wordplay can be (an) exclusive (performance): "Watch this. See if you can get it, see if you can get what I mean." Wordplay can, in this way, close down meaning. But wordplay can also be performative—a generous performance that invites others in by opening up meaning(s). Wordplay can make meaning in/visible: More visible. Less visible. Wordplay can make multiple meaning(s) (im)possible.

Wordplay is tangled. Wordplay can further tangle, just as it can be an offer to untangle. Meaning. A trip through the tangle. A trip. Through. The tangle. The construction of a sentence, the placement of words, of signs and signifiers—the wording—can intentionally trip. The reader. In wordplay, the words play differently on the page. The words play. Differently. On the page. In ways that make different meanings available to the reader/writer/reader. So, while wordplay is, itself, a form of tripping or stumbling, it is a tripping or stumbling-toward-meaning, *differently*. A trip or a stumble is thus an opportunity. An invitation. In/to learning. To read our own writing, *as-if* for the first time. As if we were learning. For the first time. Differently. Each time.

Wordplay is an opportunity, then, to reconfigure reading and writing. (And also learning and teaching.) To see how our lines and our lives are tangled, separated by a fine line only. A fine line between reading and writing. Ourselves. Learning and teaching. Our selves. In practice and in theory. The more we play with words, the more we bring the awareness of wordplay forward into our practice. The more conscious we become of the play of words, the more time we spend "playing" (where playing is a paying attention to) with words—the more we bring the practice of wordplay forward into our awareness. The familiar becomes strange becomes familiar. The kind of stumbling with words which we so often wish to avoid in our writing can, in this way, become purposeful.

Despite the ways that wordplay might create possibilities for new conditions of learning and the making of pedagogical insight, I continue to worry about wordplay. Worry that some might grow weary of wordplay before all possible meanings have been played out. I wonder whether it is possible to invite others to become serious about wordplay. To re-cognize the pedagogical possibilities in the work of wordplay. Re-cognize the tangle through wordplay. Recognize the tangle in wordplay. To recognize that wordplay is a significant part of the experience of living a life that includes the practice of writing. Knowing that wordplay is tangled. That wordplay is itself tangled. Knowing also that the tangle involves wordplay. "Somehow knowing"...the tangle is the play of words...*the tangle is itself wordplay... the tangle is itself...*

* * *

To return to the writing. Of this book. To return to (the theory and practice of) writing the tangle...I have attempted with varying degrees of success to learn to live well with the tangle, knowing—at least at an intellectual level—that as a time of working with/in and through the tangle, the writing cannot extricate itself to gaze upon the objects of its inquiry (Davis 1996). I have "known" that the tangle would be like this without knowing what the tangle would be, or how I would be made different by it. In a hermeneutic sense, I am always already re-cognizing the tangle, knowing I am inextricably part of its relations. The tangled relations: They/we are familiar. As David Jardine (1995b) notes,

> this commonplace, lived familiarity is a fascinating phenomenon because it suggests that, prior to any deliberate and methodological "educational inquiry," we find ourselves somehow already in relation ...already sharing in a complex, ambiguous, often unvoiced understanding of the constitution of the community of teaching. (105)

So while I have always been familiar at some level with the tangle, and while my intention has always been to enact a kind of research that might honor the tangle, I am still and always un/familiar with the tangle—with what might happen next. My attempts to live well with the tangle in a methodological sense do not translate well to a "method." Following Jardine (1995b) further into the tangle,

> Interpretation seeks out its affinity to its "topic." One does not have "interpretation" in hand as a method and then go out looking for a topic...Rather, something becomes a topic only when its interpretive potency strikes us. (110)

In some senses, I thought I had found the tangle and wanted to "use it" as a way to interpret "the lived features of the community of teaching and the wonders and difficulties of student-teaching they bespeak" (Jardine 1995b, 105). Now, I am struck by the tangle, recognizing that it has found me. Startled by how un/familiar it has become/is becoming. Hermeneutics is itself tangled. *The tangle is itself hermeneutic...*

I remain, meantime, particularly (self-) conscious of being lost in the tangle, unable to write my way through the tangle, unable to sort or explain it—for myself or others in a satisfactory way. To reiterate, re-cognizing the tangle at an intellectual level has not helped me to know the tangle. Thus, my reading of my own experience of writing research (and researching writing) feels, at times, unsatisfactory in the sense that I feel a certain pedagogical responsibility for understanding and for explicating my understandings—for wanting to untangle the tangle.

Before going further, it is important to note that the "making of insight," I am self-reflexively attempting to articulate here, at least as Britzman and Pitt, through Anna Freud refer to it, is not simply a matter of reflection. As Britzman and Pitt (1996) note:

> At first glance, this investigation [of the nature of learning and teaching] may seem reminiscent of reflective practice. But the nature and subject of the reflection—in terms of the time it spans and the preoccupations encouraged—is something other than a linear recall of a specific interaction or lesson...something different than the impulse to correct what is taken as a problem. (117)

That is, the tangle does not present a problem to practice, only an opportunity to problematize practice, to become implicated in the problematics of learning to practice (to write or teach, or to teach writing, and, even to write teaching). Shoshana Felman (1987) describes it further:

> This new mode of investigation and learning has...a very different temporality from the conventional linear—cumulative and progressive—temporality of learning, as it has traditionally been conceived by pedagogical theory and practice. Proceeding not through linear progression but through breakthroughs, leaps, discontinuities, regressions, and deferred action, the [psycho]analytic learning process puts in question the traditional pedagogical belief in intellectual perfectibility, the progressivist view of learning as a simple one-way road from ignorance to knowledge. (76)

Breakthroughs. Leaps. *Discontinuities.* Regressions. *Deferred action.* Through some or all of these, the making of insight becomes more than simply gaining (a)(new) understanding(s) of what this research project (and, in turn, this tangle) is *about*; it is, rather, an understanding of a different order, an insight that implicates me in my own learning. The making of insight concerns the nature of how I am made different by my engagement with the research itself. By how I am. Made. Different. As Felman (1987) suggests,

> the significance of the discovery appears only in retrospect, because insight is never purely cognitive; it is to some extent always performative (incorporated in an act, a doing) and to that extent precisely it is not transparent to itself. Insight is partially unconscious, partially partaking of a practice. And since there can never be a simultaneous, full coincidence between practice and awareness, what one understands in doing and through doing appears in retrospect...(15)

This "new" insight, then, in which I am "suddenly" aware of the tangle in all its relations in (a) distinctly different way(s), feels like a discovery, a sudden glimpse into knowing. The glimpse, however, is itself a tangling as it shows me writing the tangle. Performing the tangle, where insight and understanding "are always performative—always a strategy for constructing knowledge" (Ellsworth 1996, 139). It is a *writing* of the tangle as I am written by it, where writing—and learning and researching— are (always) a sometimes-stumbling to/ward the making of insight. I am, in this way, always having to make insight in/through practice—the practice of writing, or researching, or teaching—always having to perform it, even though I am not always aware, not always knowing, where the performance is leading or even what it is I am performing. I must (always) discover (the making of) insight in order to bring my (new/er) awareness forward into practice, as well as bring my (re)new(ed) practice forward into awareness, because, to repeat Felman's words, "what one understands in doing and through doing appears in retrospect" (15). The resulting performance is itself (a) tangle(d). *The tangle is itself performative...*

Interesting, how I seem to have un/consciously positioned myself in a place—a location—which *is* a tangle. Or, to go a step further, I have not only discovered myself in a position of tangle, I have also discovered that I have enacted, have been enacting—will always be enacting the tangle as a location from which to consider the conditions of a life that includes the practice of writing, of teaching, of theorizing writing and teaching—of researching the theory and practice of writing (and) pedagogy. Practicing and theorizing—writing—pedagogy. *Writing* pedagogy.

Q: Can the tangle be conceptualized?
A: The tangle is itself conceptual, it both invites and resists conceptualization. In this way the tangle is an invitation to resistance, an invitation that resists, a resistance that is inviting...

Turning the Tangle into a Curiosity— Turning Curiosity into a Tangle

The curious time of pedagogy is the time of knowing too much and learning too little, of being too early and too late. (Britzman 1998, 135)

Can a study of the self studying education create new conditions for learning and the making of pedagogical insight? Without knowing, without being aware of my knowing, this question has been moving through these words, through this work, moving it forward. And backward. Visibly and invisibly. As Britzman and Pitt (1996) describe it, "casting learning backward and forward and providing more space [for me] to consider [my own] conflicts in learning" (123). In this way, the writing of this research continues to teach me what the research is about: *a study of the self studying education.* Creating new conditions of learning that enable me to continue to bring my awareness forward into practice as well as to bring my practice forward into awareness. The research is always already a "writing toward awareness."[1]

I write the research(-as-tangle metaphor)[2] not simply to point out how the experience of writing—in this case about a life that

---

[1] I borrow Ellsworth's notion of "reading toward awareness" from "Situated Response-ability to Student Papers (1996)," which I refer to often in this chapter.
[2] In an earlier draft of the book, written some time ago, this sentence was written: "I make use of the research-as-tangle metaphor." I have now changed it, significantly, to "I write the research(-as-tangle metaphor)," because of the

includes the writing of lives—is tangled, though this has certainly been true of my experience. The tangle, of writing and teaching and learning, is, of course, marked by uncertainty and pratfalls, full of twists and turns. I also want more than to show how this research work re-presents a time of learning/living—for myself and for those whose lives are re-presented here—that is full of ambivalence and charged with resistance; tangled. Following Britzman (1998), I strive to show how such anxiety and ambivalence and resistance—with/in and through the tangle —become pedagogical—in Britzman's terms, how "resistance to learning must be made into a curiosity; to learn from resistance...ambivalence...must be tolerated (1998, 134)."[3] Thus, "[w]hat becomes pedagogical is the possibility of learners implicating themselves in their learning" (Britzman and Pitt 1996, 117).

The curious time of pedagogy, then, finds me implicated, deeply, in a learning that is mine and not mine. I am implicated in the sense in which the word means to fold or twist together. Intertwine. Tangle. Consider the practice of writing: Research; a Self; research of a Self writing. A self writing research that includes other selves. Writing.

The curious time of pedagogy is a time of considering what the implications might be of not knowing what you know. Or, not knowing that you know. This is the disturbing nature of knowing itself. This startle—this involuntary start—the sudden recognition of not knowing sets knowing in motion, causes a ripple. The involuntary aspect of being startled suggests that there are things going on that are somehow independent of our will, unintentional. Unconscious. There is knowing beyond our awareness. Knowing beyond our knowing. Knowing that doesn't know itself. Knowing that doesn't know it knows itself.

---

discovery through the making of insight, that the tangle is no longer a metaphor, at least one that is mine to "make use of." The bracketing, more than wordplay, signifies the ways that "writing the research" is (also) writing the tangle which also means being written by the tangle, being written by the research.

[3] All of the Britzman (1998) citations are taken from a talk given at UBC on July 16, 1996, by Deborah Britzman entitled, "That Lonely Discovery: Anne Frank, Anna Freud and the Question of Pedagogy," which has since become a chapter in *Lost subjects, contested objects* (1998).

In the context of teacher education, the notion that knowing is in some way "beyond us," out of our control can be the source of further disturbance to our understanding of how we teach. How we learn to teach. How we learn. It suggests instead, contrary to many of our pedagogical assumptions, that learning to teach has more to do with learning to learn. Teaching and learning are in this way, profoundly connected. (As well as profoundly tangled.) Bringing this insight forward into awareness: teaching is a form of learning. This insight begs the question of how we might then bring this awareness forward into practice. Following the work of educators like Felman (1987), Britzman (1991; 1998), Britzman and Pitt (1996), Ellsworth (1996), and Pitt (1996), who bring psychoanalytic insight to bear on pedagogy, we might be best served by attending to the disturbing conditions that our learning makes available to us, pay attention to the ways in which we are disturbed by our own learning.

Britzman (1998) makes an important case for educators to begin to acknowledge learning as a psychic event "charged with resistance to knowledge." This resistance, however, as Britzman notes, is a "precondition for learning from knowledge and the grounds of knowledge itself." This, of course, is yet another sense in which pedagogy—and its relations—are tangled. The work of Felman, Britzman, and others does not suggest that we begin to understand pedagogy as a dynamic that is tangled. Rather, it suggests that we acknowledge that pedagogy is itself tangled, and, further, that *the tangle is itself pedagogic*; that is, it becomes pedagogic as we "make pedagogy"[4] through the tangle by beginning to acknowledge what Britzman terms the deep attachment to and implication in knowledge. (Jardine, in a hermeneutic rendering, might suggest that learning trails dark and chaotic attachments, entrails that require our attendings.)

This psychoanalytic insight points to the ways that *learning is itself tangled*. Like hermeneutic interpretation, psychoanalytic practice and theory point to the rich and troubling ambiguity, as

---

[4] The phrase "making pedagogy" seems a rather crude construction but I am somehow compelled to use it as a way of implicating myself in my own messy learning of the tangle, my own messy tangle of learning. I use it, loosely, as the equivalent of the making of pedagogical insight that continues to echo through this chapter by way of the opening epigram by Britzman and Pitt (1996).

well as the dynamic complexity of pedagogy. This "learning of a different order" suggests that the making of insight comes from a provocation. There is something "at stake" in this kind of learning as it disturbs us, disturbs our (psychological) self—our psyche—and, in turn, our understanding is irrevocably changed. As Felman (1987) states, there is little room for "ready-made interpretations, for knowledge given in advance" (81); rather it is part of a "dramatic pedagogical performance" (73) that is enacted as we spend time with each other in classrooms.

In their provocative essay, "Pedagogy and Transference: Casting the Past of Learning into the Presence of Teaching (1996)," which I have been drawing upon as an important source, Deborah Britzman and Alice Pitt state:

> In thinking about our work with beginning teachers, we have become curious about *the shift* from a preoccupation with teaching other people to teach to a consideration of the conditions for one's own learning. (1996, 117, emphasis mine)

In the process of becoming willingly tangled with/in this "shift"—for the ways I might be made different by attending to some of the "internal conflicts" that structure some of my own patterns of learning, I have, at times, questioned, resisted, the strong pull of self-reflexivity required to attend to this "difficult knowledge" (Britzman 1998). Perhaps, it has been the fear of being swallowed by self-reflexivity and thus losing sight of the "other" selves—the teacher candidates—whose writing lives I am living in relation with/to. (And, perhaps it is also for fear of re-cognizing myself.) Britzman and Pitt (1996), themselves, ask:

> What does it mean to bring this [psychoanalytic] demand to pedagogy? We accept this question knowing the vulnerabilities it poses for those learning to teach and for those already teaching. From the vantage of newcomers, such an odd demand seems to be asking student teachers to forget about their students and to reduce all engagements to the psychological self. (118)

Learning and teaching, self and other, seem to be caught up in the tangle. Through the tangle, they become visible, then invisible, then visible. As learning and teaching approach one another, as each becomes less distinct, the tangle opens out into all its (tangled) relations. Britzman (1998) describes the complexity of the pedagogical dynamic in this way: "learning, it turns out, is crafted from a curious set of relations—the self's relation to its own otherness and the self's relation to the other's otherness (134)." When we come together to learn, in this case within the context of teacher education, we become part of a complex dynamic in which knowledge, or knowing is not a "substance" that can be transmitted or gathered in our efforts to mean but is, rather, a "structural dynamic" that we enter in to. Psychoanalytic insight (like hermeneutics) thus lends itself to the tangle—of learning and teaching—as a way of learning to live well with the difficulty of the tangle, even as it reveals the tangled nature of learning and teaching. *Psychoanalysis is itself tangled.* The tangle is itself psycho/analytic.

Judith Robertson (1997) offers helpful insight into the tangled movement of self and other, of inner and outer, in her work with teacher candidates. She helps to construct a frame for the complex process of identity negotiation that takes place through the tangle. Like Britzman and Pitt, Robertson's work involves the study of "the unconscious and its conflicts in educators, and...the role of language in mediating between conscious and subconscious realities" (Robertson 1997, 29). She describes the "unconscious... as a set of dynamics that structure the psyche and social lives of all human beings in unexpectedly significant ways"...and, further,..."how the inner lives and learning of beginning teachers relate—at least through language use—to the external worlds of teaching" (29).

This connection of "inner" and "outer," of psyche and social, is a significant connection for me in and through the tangle of identity negotiation, for the ways it implicates the tangle as a location for "the psychic work of making identity" (Pitt 1996, 38). The tangle, then, becomes a place of crisis for the negotiation of identity. A place of negotiation for the crisis of identity. The tangle, borrowing the words of Sumara and Luce-Kapler (1996), offers "a location for self-interpretation" (77). Following Sumara and Luce-Kapler's (1996) work on "negotiating identities while learning to teach," a sense of self-identity does not really have a fixed location inside the body of the individual but, rather, is ambiguously located amid the human subject's perceived and interpreted relations in the world...a sense of self or communal identity is not stable, continuous or fixed. Identity cannot be contained within immutable categories. (69)

So a recognition and acknowledgment of the study of the self studying education, in fact, creates new conditions for learning that allow for the making of pedagogical insight—through the tangle: a self studying selves studying selves studying education. It would, of course, be unimaginable to consider questions of teacher candidates' negotiations of identity without re-considering my own. Identity negotiation is itself tangled. *The tangle is itself an identity negotiation*...I can't see from only one location. I am multiply located. I am located in the tangle which is neither here nor there. Neither this nor that.

Through the tangle, I recognize that identity is always and already tangled, and that the time of learning, "the time of pedagogy" is, as Britzman and Pitt have said, a "casting the time of learning backward and forward" (1996, 122). The curious time of pedagogy is a con-fuse-ing (of) time. In a tangled way, self and other become necessarily con/fused. The tangle, however, enables us to remain curious about this shift in the focus of teacher education, from the central question of "How do we teach (other) people to teach?" to "How do people learn?" (Britzman et al. 1995, 2); it enables us to remain curious about the ways that learning and teaching, self and other, are always con/fusing.

The ENED 426 experience, in hindsight, was about becoming curious about this shift from a "preoccupation" to a "con-sideration." [As a sidebar: the use of the word "preoccupation" makes for an interesting pedagogical play on words when the context is the talk of teacher education. A pre-occupation, for example, might be something we experience before occupying the place of teacher, the anxiety we experience as we consider taking on the occupation of teaching.] We want to learn about teaching. We want to know how to teach. Although there is always much talk of learning in teacher education, we tend to focus on teaching in ways that, in an ironic sense, often leaves our own learning (as teachers) unexplored. We want to know enough about teaching in order to feel secure enough to teach. We want to know everything first, learn it, so that we can be in charge of learning. We tend to concentrate on how we can help our students learn in ways that ensure that we won't be put in the awkward or vulnerable place of "learner" ourselves. We thus avoid implicating ourselves. Our own learning goes uninterrogated, undisturbed.

As Britzman et al. (1995) claim, teacher education programs organized around the question of teaching people to teach, shut out "consideration of more complex conversations about what conflictive forms of knowledge, identity, community, language and its practices might mean in education" (2). Questions of teaching people to teach do not acknowledge the tangle. As I understand it, then, leaving (the word) "teaching" out of conversations that attempt to address some of our most fundamental concerns as educators works, paradoxically, to open up "unprecedented teaching possibilities, renewing both the questions and the practice of education" (Felman 1987, 70).

Britzman's earlier work in *Practice Makes Practice* (1991) provides a particularly insightful account of the contradictory realities "that beckon and disturb" those learning to teach (2). In examining the ways teachers come to construct teaching identities, she illustrates "how systemic constraints become lived as individual dilemmas" (3). In constructing "the student teacher as the site of conflict," Britzman foregrounds the messy problematics of learning to teach—what Jo Anne Pagano (1990) has referred to as "the conundrum of identification" in teacher education—where "taking up an identity means suppressing aspects of the self" (Britzman 1991, 4). Of course, postmodern notions of identity do much to confound, conflate, celebrate and de/construct our understandings of self. As Paula Salvio (1996) notes, "the de-lineation of a self too often demands the exclusion or expulsion of other possible selves" (3). So we might interpret Britzman's state-ment about "suppressing aspects of the self" as a suppression of certain selves in favor of other selves in the complex process of identity negotiation involved in becoming a teacher. As I continue to bring psychoanalytic insight to bear upon my own project of learning to become curious about lives that include the practice of writing, the attempt to conceptualize the tangle is, as Britzman (1998) states, "the work of teacher education—our work in teacher education; it is the conceptual work we are ethically obligated to do, not on the students but on ourselves." She continues, "the students will learn with or without us. We can create good conditions for learning but what that learning is about is the students' own." My choosing to frame the task of pedagogy through the tangle is an attempt to show how writing practice that involves wordmaking, poetrymaking and theorymaking might "create new conditions for learning and to observe the learning provoked as an effect of these conditions" (Britzman and Pitt 1996, 120).

Situated Pedagogy:
Classroom Practices in Postmodern Times

> ... to teach in such a moment when familiar categories break down in the face of the complexities of lived lives...(Lather and Ellsworth 1996, 70)

Can a study of the self studying education create new conditions of learning and the making of pedagogical insight? This question, which continues to haunt this chapter is itself situated, in part, in the midst of the pedagogical practice of two particular educators (Britzman and Pitt) who attempt to use psychoanalytic theory and practice to inform educational practice and theory. Further, their practice, articulated in an essay which I have returned to often, comes from the middle of a series of essays (mentioned at the outset in *"a very large footnote with an 'I' for form"*) in a special issue of *Theory into Practice (TIP)* which I now believe is an issue dedicated to the tangle; an issue positioned with/in the tangle. Patti Lather and Elizabeth Ellsworth, the issue's editors, suggest that each of the articles are connected through

> a conviction that the resources for finding our way in the postmodern moment lie in learning to look closely into the dense particularities of concrete situations of teaching and learning rather than more generalized calls for one sort of classroom practice or another. (1996, 70)

Lather and Ellsworth continue,

> While there is much debate as to what the postmodern is, it signals both the proliferation of...differences and the sense that we live between the

no longer and the not yet, a time when formerly comfortable holds on making sense of the world no longer suffice. (70)

In a thoroughly "postmodern moment," David Schaasfma (1996) talks about the postmodern moment by citing Brenda Marshall (1992) (who "originally" coined the phrase "the postmodern moment,") who says that postmodernism "is about the threads that we trace but never to conclusion" (Marshall, cited in Schaasfma, 1996, 115). Schaasfma, also a contributor to the special *Theory into Practice* issue, then continues,

> I might argue that many if not all moments in my classroom are essentially postmodern in this respect: Examined closely, they are all excessive of the possibility of single explanations. They have—if they become the object of critical exploration and continued performance...the potential to lead to an endless exploration of possibilities, instead of the dull and dangerous moment of final conclusions. (115)

The postmodern (moment), as I continue to understand and enact it, is lived through the tangle—and in the tangle. The postmodern moment is itself tangled. *The tangle is itself postmodern.* Consider this tangle of words I have purposefully created that come from a number of educators—in this case from the *TIP* special issue (1996)—who attempt to work in and through the postmodern moment, where sense is made without certainty (of knowing):

> I have tried to push at the borders of socially sanctioned pedagogical strategies through the blending of theory, spectatorship, performance and memory work. I have seriously rethought the pedagogical forms I utilize and have attempted to teach in ways that simultaneously construct and deconstruct knowledge claims—in my ever-changing positions as teacher, adviser, spectator, occasional co-producer, and audience member...**My hope is that the stories I tell will provide readers with opportunities to recognize some of the insights, silences, ambiguities, and masks in their own teaching stories as they become aware of the insights, silences, masks, and ambiguities that inhabit mine**...There are places for ambiguity, paradox, debate, serious doubts, laughter, and irony in stories that other genres and forms do not generally permit...**With this collection, then, we do not set out to prescribe actual situated pedagogies that we expect educators to replicate in their own practice. Rather, we want to offer educators**

contextualized analyses of actual classroom dilemmas and
demonstrate the strategic understandings that situated analysis makes
possible (Orner 1996, 72–73; **Berlak 1996, 93;** Schaafsma 1996, 112;
Lather and Ellsworth 1996, 71).

Reading many of the essays in the special (spring 1996) issue
of *TIP* has helped me to discover a way of positioning my own
work within a framework offered by the title of the *Theory into
Practice* issue: "Situated Pedagogies: Classroom Practices in
Postmodern Times." My choice to re-present the tangled manner
in which each of these essays come together and apart in a form
that plays with words, begins to enact the ways I am approaching
the tangle, choosing to be with the tangle. It is not a better way,
just one way of attempting to live in the tangle, write the tangle.
To be written by the tangle. A tangled theory of practice, a tangled
practice of theory. The forms that seem to best suit the tangle are
ones that (enable me) to perform the tangle: Wordplay that begins
to play at poetry. The tangle is not pre-formed, it must be performed...

By way of writing process—of the particulars of the writing
and researching of this book—much of the historic wrestling I
have done with, and in, the tangle has been a moving toward and
a moving away from some kind of analysis of an "actual
classroom dilemma" for fear of mis-representing the tangle (of the
classroom). For fear of not being able to say what happened, and, I
suppose, for fear of saying what 'actually' happened. For fear of
not saying enough. Or saying too much. Much of my own inner
conflict—my dilemma of how to re-present a particular classroom
practice—has im/balanced on the attraction/resistance of
somehow creating a model of that practice (which most often risks
mis-interpretation as a "model practice.") I dwelled, often, in a
place of angst, worrying in/over the hyphenated spaces of my
multiple roles as researcher and teacher and writer and student.
Researcher-teacher-writer-student. This conflated identity, which
has been writing me as I have been writing it, has often left me
feeling ill-suited and ambivalent toward the task of somehow
offering an interpretation of a particular pedagogical experience—of somehow re-presenting pedagogy in the form of
research: bringing my attention inward to a study of a six-week
pedagogical experience and, then, outward to "translating," or

"transforming," or turning this attention toward some form of representation left me wanting for ways to enact/perform, in Felman's terms, "the lived experience of a discovery" (1987, 4). It seems I wanted to enact a research—to perform something I had yet to discover. My "dilemma" as a researcher, then, was much like the dilemma I often experience in writing; this is the experience in which I must write in order to convey my thoughts/ideas/feelings/understandings, yet I cannot know what they are until I have written them. So it was with my research which could only be discovered through my researching, which, as I will argue in chapter 5, is simply another form of writing.

In the absence of this particular (making of) pedagogical insight, which I am only discovering now—in and through the latter stages of writing—I experienced what I might call a more stereotypical research dilemma, namely, how to "do research" on a particular lived experience made up of a complex set of elements, both visible and invisible, without reducing its complexity or rendering it somehow inert in the process. What to do with all these data? Why all these data? What mattered? What would be worthy of doing? How to justify my research choices and my reasons for researching and re-presenting a particular experience to a particular scholarly community (and to myself and the teacher candidates)?

Throughout the time leading up to, including, and then following the six-week pedagogical experience of the ENED 426 course, I continued, consciously and unconsciously, to resist any one "method" of research again, in this particular case, in order to avoid holding the experience up as a "model pedagogy." (That is, I somehow knew that something of pedagogical value had occurred. The teacher candidates (and I) loved the course and seemed to learn and grow as learners and writers and teachers in important and powerful ways. What was happening here? Others should know about this. How can I tell them about it?) Following this line of reasoning, my research would have endeavored to re-present whatever model I discovered/developed. Trouble is, this process seemed to itself require a "model research." A model that would somehow anticipate and address any and all methodological concerns/dilemmas so that the research itself would not interfere with the pedagogy modelled; a model that, once finished, would have no leftover pieces remaining. As Jardine has stated, in hermeneutic interpretive terms, this model longs "for the last word...[where] nothing more will need to be said" (1992c, 118). Or, as Felman (1987) articulates through a psychoanalytic lens, a model, would lead to "the exhaustion—through methodological investigation—of all there is to know" (77).

As Britzman and Pitt (1996) note, "models in education" suggest there are "discrete models 'out there' that one merely picks up then applies" (119); noting our historic and inbred tendencies in teacher education programs to offer such models, they suggest—with wonderful irony and serious intent—that we might be better served by teacher education courses (and by our research of those courses) that explore and interrogate "strange" models in education—"models" that "instead provide contexts of learning where one might become interested in the problematics of learning" (119).

Model pedagogy and research, then, were obviously not the way to go. It seemed that no amount of reflection would provide the necessary opening to "the invisibles."[5] Yet I had difficulty envisioning the alternatives. I created a binary for myself by holding up "a model" as one possibility versus a, a what? (I couldn't say what might exist in its stead.) A critique? An undoing? An unbiased reporting? I had not yet identified the tangle, but I already knew that I was "in it" and framing it would be inadvisable, if not impossible given the knowledge of which I had such a limited working awareness.

The articulation of the researching of situated pedagogical practices by Lather and Ellsworth (1996), as well as by the other authors contributing to *TIP*, offered ways to begin to live and write and research (from within) the tangle. They helped me to address my question of how to "do research" when everything is always and already tangled; it was, as Patti Lather offers in *Getting Smart*, the beginnings of a way to research and "write postmodern...to simultaneously use and call into question a

---

[5] In his most recent book *The Soul's Code*, James Hillman (1996) asks, "What is the relationship between what we see and what we don't ?...What means are there for transporting the unseen into the seen? Or the seen into the unseen?" (94–95).

discourse, to both challenge and inscribe dominant meaning systems in ways that construct our own categories and frameworks as contingent, positioned, partial" (1990, 1).

To simultaneously use and call into question...to both challenge and inscribe. Lather's words offered ways to begin to read my own experience—of researching the experience of "others"—as a writing toward awareness; Lather's words were a window. Of confirmation. Of the need to dwell with the ENED 426 experience in particular ways. In particular. Situated. In what Ellsworth and Lather—echoing Bronwen Wallace's notion of the stubborn particulars—call the materials present in the unique particulars of the moment.

"The Lived Experience of a Discovery": Wordmaking. Poetrymaking. Theorymaking.

> To me...theory emerges from the concrete, from my efforts to makes sense of everyday life experiences, from my efforts to intervene critically in my life and the lives of others. (hooks 1994, 70)

The tangle is both generous and generative. It offers new possibilities for students and teachers—learners and learners—to be together in classrooms creating conditions that enable curricular acts of reading and writing to flourish. Ellsworth (1996) talks about "a shift from producing a reading to becoming curious about *how* we read..." (141). I, of course, am interested in making this same shift *from producing a writing to becoming curious about how we write*...Writing is performative. Like reading, "It makes something happen" (141).

Within the context of teacher education, the value of (researching) writing practice, as I have attempted to enact it in this chapter, is not only in its offer of further practice—of writing to learn (about writing and about teaching)—but also in its offer of a location where the tangle itself might be workshopped. Performed. That is, the focus—in writing and in teaching—is not necessarily on "finding" learning or understanding but on the process of entertaining the particulars that make the place between knowing and not-knowing so pedagogically rich. I believe the ENED 426 classroom offered such a location, where writing practice created new conditions of learning and the making of pedagogical insight—a place between practice and awareness in which to enact/perform knowing and not knowing. Knowing and not knowing enacted. Through writing. Following Ellsworth's insights into reading practice, writing practice offers a way of placing the responsibility for writing, and for writings made, with the writers and "the uses they intend to make of the knowledge and sense they construct" (1996, 140). (Some of these particulars will be taken up in chapter 6.)

Again, looking to the work of the educators who have sought to both endorse and problematize classroom practice through situated pedagogies (Schaafsma 1996), writing "process" takes on newer and potentially deeper meaning and implication as a process that is also part of "the continuing struggle to become aware" (Felman, in Ellsworth 1996, 143). The writing workshop, as I continue to reconceptualize it in the context of teacher education, offers opportunities to employ writing practice that brings poetry and pedagogy together in productive juxtaposition for the ways they might "mutually inform—and displace—each other" (Felman 1987, 49). Poetry and pedagogy. Here, I do not refer necessarily to the poetry of pedagogy, nor to the pedagogy of poetry but, rather, how each might teach us to read the other and ourselves. In so doing, the work of poetry and pedagogy and, in turn, the work of teacher education "is not necessarily to recognize a *known*, to find an answer, but also, and perhaps more challengingly, to locate an *unknown*, to find a question" (Felman 1987, 49). Poetry and pedagogy, together and alone, offer the possibility of enabling us to "take in and absorb more than [we] know"(5). As an embodied footnote, it is again important to announce my "discovery," along with teacher candidates, of some of the ways that wordplay can become poetry within the generous location of the workshop. In our ongoing curricular interpretations, wordplay is becoming (of) poetry. Wordplay is also becoming (of) pedagogy.

The tangle as I continue to conceptualize it, offers opportunities for those in teacher education to recast their work together as human beings engaged in acts of reading and writing through the possibilities—individually and in community—of "a lived experience of discovery" (Felman 1987, 4). The workshop-styled classroom foregrounds this shift in responsibility for the ways in which we might conceptualize reading and writing as curious acts that are "not intended to be used, not 'understood'—grasped fully, generically, or directly, once and for all" (Ellsworth 1996, 141). Writing practice, then, offers opportunities to continually *write* practice. Said another way, writing practice enables us to continue to practice writing as a way of creating further possibilities for practice so that practice never stops writing us and we never stop writing practice.

My own writing practice, which includes the writing of this research, continues to enable me to engage in my own "struggle to become aware," to write toward a greater awareness of the shared experience of six weeks lived together in a course that included the practice of writing. My feelings are akin to Ellsworth's when she states, "this pedagogical practice is still new and unfamiliar to me. The meanings of it as a pedagogical practice are not transparent...[then, she quotes Felman, as I too have quoted Felman], there is never a *full coincidence between practice and awareness*" (1996, 143).

Throughout the ENED 426 experience, the emphasis was not necessarily on teacher candidates becoming poets or even better writers, but rather it was on a practice that enabled them to begin to know themselves through wordmaking and wordplay (which we sometimes chose to call poetry). The practice of writing was a way to explore and address some of our anxieties, conflicts, and desires—of learning to write and learning to teach, and most important, of learning to learn. ENED 426 was, in these kinds of ways, not a "rush to application,"[6] not a practice of learning language across the curriculum (as I believe some of the other sections of the course may have been, despite being well intentioned in their pedagogies). The rush to write (language) across the curriculum would only have masked anxieties of how much we wanted to be/come teachers who knew how to write across the curriculum. In Britzman's (1998) terms, this would have only involved a learning *about* language across the curriculum. Writing practice better enabled us to become more

---

[6] Britzman et al. (1995) talk about the "rush to apply" as a disturbing "syndrome" within Faculties of Education in which "experience is reduced to a technical problem of classroom application" (4).

aware—more curious—about this rush to application and how it affected our writing practice and, in turn, how writing practice influenced the rush to application.

Writing practice—through the tangle—whether it is a book or a poem or a life—is the practice of creating conditions that enable one to continue to practice *writing* practice, to continue theorizing the practice of writing—a book or a poem or a life. Writing—to learn—becomes a life practice.

* * *

Q: What is the experience of living a life that includes the practice of writing?

A: It is an experience of en-tangle-ment.[7]

---

[7] It is the experience of finding out what the tangle-meant. Of attempting to find out what living in the tangle-meant, only to find that the tangle never meant one thing, never meant to tangle but always means to tangle. The tangle is not a means to an end but rather a means to a tangle. A tangle means...

taking attendance:
an absence of comment

_____ **INTERLUDE**

Miscellaneous Preservice Teacher Comments
(Re-presented by Their Absence)

The following preservice teacher comments are (re)present(ed) by their absence. I make a deliberate choice to include this "blank" space not so much as a clever-minded postmodern performance—a waste of paper even—but, rather, as a way of offering up my ambivalent and often empty feelings of dissatisfaction at how little I really heard in the classroom; it is also a plain-faced lament for how horribly distorted the amplification of such a tiny signal can potentially become.

For me, the following dedicated space re-presents another attempt at a respectful listening—a moment of textual silence to once again imagine the tangle of lives—this time without words...

taking attendance:
all present

_____ INTERLUDE

Miscellaneous Preservice Teacher Comments
(Re-presented by Their Presence)

Comments from "exit slips" of Teacher Candidates:

...I feel guilty about my reluctance to work with my group, my involuntary reaction to withdraw and to not participate. What if my own students feel this way? How do we, as teachers, choose groups? What about my own belief in acceptance, kindness, and understanding? The week has been interesting, disquieting, inspirational, and thought-provoking. For my money, what more could I ask for? We've dealt with issues that will affect my teaching career...

...I am amazed at how I view things from a teacher's perspective. I am always using what I learn to try and apply it to teaching. This class provides me with a lot of tools...

...I felt some dis-ease this morning when faced with writing the theme of "love" into a memo...I laughed with many of the others in class but afterward I realized what I was laughing at...It wasn't funny anymore...

...Convention: What new ways can we create to tell stories? Can we reject the market-oriented-popular-culture way? Do those who call out not need agreement of values? What happens to conflicting conventions?...

...Wild mind died when the monkeys started chattering. The mind was quicker than the hand...

...As a suggestion—could you give us the order in which we should really read the chapters in the book?...

E-mail excerpts:

Date: Thu, 23 May 1996 20:53:51 -0700 (PDT)
To: rasberry@unixg.ubc.ca
Subject: poets?

Do we become poets, having never been poets, or do we rediscover a former self, ability, or openness that had been lost?

Date: Thu, 24 May 1996 8:33:32 -0700 (PDT)
To: rasberry@unixg.ubc.ca
Subject: magic formula

What makes a class work? Though there is no magic formula, I think part of the reason that this class works is student ownership, teacher respect, and being "allowed" to express our …"selves." It is a mutual trust and sharing. How we create that is to be both a guide and open to the desires of our class. To create a classroom is also to create a state of mind. We as teachers are "learning junkies," we should share that addiction versus forcing a specific agenda. It takes time with kids though. The transformation that has occurred in our class would take more time with kids. Remember it is "US" and "THEM," maybe that is the formula, changing that perspective into "WE." Noble thoughts, eh! I am going to miss this class, simply for what it has sparked and what it generates. Where others have grumbled, we have laughed. How to replicate…share the laughter…share the "WE"…

Date: Thu, 23 May 1996 20:53:51 -0700 (PDT)
To: rasberry@unixg.ubc.ca
Subject: risk

426 was about so many things. Poetry and writing a journal, etc. are things taught in English courses but one of the differences was that Carl lives the life of a poet so all that stuff we did was very personal and real…So being invited to be a poet is partly

showing what that world is about through someone who lives it, experiencing some level of creativity that isn't the norm, taking the risk as Carl invited us to do with regard to marks, the recognition from others on our endeavors. I guess what this invitation has to do with becoming a teacher is being open minded, taking risks, putting your own mark on the job, and in turn giving the same thing back to your students whatever the subject, in my case inviting the students to find the joy and power in mastering math by doing some of the same things. I've seen some take that invitation and many that haven't. All you can do is put your heart into it and hope for the best. Unfortunately, I don't think I succeeded in doing that for Mary (the singer), so I hope to grow and get better at teaching...Meantime, this poetry is burning a hole in my binder...

CHAPTER FIVE

The Curious Time of Researching Pedagogy

There is neither day nor night, but rather a continual dawning.

—James Hillman, *Puer papers*, 1979.

A continual dawning; this seems a rather apt way to begin to characterize, as well as complicate, teaching and learning and our talk of teaching and learning. If pedagogy were a painting, such a canvas would—"in the moment of passing...likely have more power to stop us than we would have power to walk on" (Winterson 1996, 3). The allure of such light seems full of promise—enough to keep the palette fat-with-color in anticipation of seeing the never-before-seen. As Madeleine Grumet—truly a curricular artist—has said about the fine line that separates/connects the beautiful mundane work of teaching, "All that we need to decide, each day, when we are ready and the light is right, is where and when to draw the line" (1988, 94). Even so, this same sense of limitless expectancy in teacher education, this open-eyed waiting, burns the eyes, dis-orients, unsettles. Neither day nor night. Charged with ambivalence, a continual dawning hardly seems sustainable. Where (and when) would we draw the line? A continual dawning, then, offers to shed a *different* sort of light on the researching of teaching and learning that is at once anxiety-provoking and hope-full.

We seem to know a lot more about (researching) the light of day in teacher education. Daylight. Day-planners that log our time together in schools. Day in, day out. The classroom is a canvas that stretches its invitation, and with the best of intentions we imagine it waits for *our* brushstroke and *our* eye for color. This is not necessarily unhappy news. The time of teacher education—when does it end?—is a time when we are dizzy with light. Pouring in through south-facing windows of the classroom, unyielding with its overhead fluorescent eye, emanating from opened books and manicured lesson plans, glaring from overhead projectors that illuminate our pedagogy with unblinking eyes. These are the familiar scenes of teaching and learning that, blinded by all this light, we imagine to be enacting for the first time; or, if not the first time, then the time when we will finally get it right. Again, this is for the most part good news. We live in teacher education with desire, wanting to get it right. Hopeful of our days together and, with the best of intentions, we situate our living in classrooms as a difficult yet worthwhile kind of living. Bringing our learning to light. Bringing light to our learning.

Nightfall, on the other hand, marks a more uncertain time for teaching and learning. Recognizable, like stars floating liquid on a dark surface: the classroom turned upside down. Extracurricular at best, avoidable if possible. The place of home-work. Answers to assignments appear back at school the next day, like magic, unquestionable. Difficult to ask questions about this time of learning. The shadows seem less invitational.

Then there is the in-between time. Neither day nor night…

My point in drawing attention to the horizon is not to suggest that we recast teacher education as a time of continual dawning; rather, it is to point to how our sense of time—in teacher education and in our educational researchings of teacher education—acts as a profound measure of everyday moments and movements, and how this sense of time consciously and unconsciously affects our enactments of teaching and learning. And researching. A continual dawning, then, offers a curious invitation…

Understood one way, a continual dawning speaks of a beginning or an opening that appears to grow light without end. This particular aspect of the light metaphor, for me, speaks to the kind of "crazy optimism" with which we most often approach our research of the work of "learning to teach," which, like much of the discourse of teacher education itself, is conducted as though all still seems possible. A central assumption that underlies this kind of discourse is that "there is a way to teach how to teach" (Britzman et al. 1995, 2) and, by extension, a *way* to research this time of teaching, this "teaching how to teach."

A continual dawning, as a strangely ambivalent metaphor for the time of researching pedagogy, also holds other possibilities for insights into our learning (to teach), as well as our researching of our learning (to teach). Becoming curious about researching pedagogy suggests we seek ways to talk with/in and about this "half-light of ambivalence" (Hillman 1989, 30), seek other ways to recast the time of research in teacher education. James Hillman argues that psychology, and I would venture to add teacher education, "usually gives to ambivalence a major pejorative judgment" (1979, 14). The practice of teacher education, and our methodological attendings to this practice seem to leave little room for uncertainty despite the acknowledged difficulty, both of learning to teach and, of learning to research our teaching. Hillman suggests, however, that ambivalence, rather than being overcome, might "be developed within its own principle. It is a way in itself...to cure away ambivalence removes the eye with which we can perceive...the paradoxes of knowing and not-knowing" (1979, 36). For Hillman, "living in ambivalence is living where yea and nay, light and darkness, right action and wrong are held closely together and are difficult to distinguish" (1979, 14).

Influenced by the work of Hillman (1979, 1989), David Jardine's (1994b) interpretive effort at "re-mythologizing pedagogy" points to the ways that our work in teacher education might benefit from a more generous—even courageous—treatment of the ambiguity and difficulty and uncertainty of the work of learning (to teach). Through the tangle. Jardine suggests that much of our pedagogical and methodological attention in teacher education tends to focus on "interventions aimed at facilitating and easing the transition" (Jardine 1994b, 17) from "student" to "teacher."

The invitation to re-consider and reconfigure ambiguity in (the research of) teacher education, following Jardine, requires that we question the idea that "every difficulty confronted is somehow avoidable" if we could only "orchestrate it well enough" (Jardine 1994b). Yes, if only we could orchestrate it well enough. If teaching and learning is, as Britzman et al. suggest, "highly specific, contextual, perspectival, constructed, and in a sense, unrepeatable" (1995, 5), then how do we begin to research it? How do we talk about teaching and learning in our roles as researchers whose very act(ion)s, in a contradictory sense, threaten to foreclose on an ongoing conversation by our insistence on speaking? How do we research the classroom *when it is always itself, restless, forever altering its color like a sad eye?*

As Jardine notes, our research of the time of teacher education must begin to

> make this difficult liminal experience readable and understandable and decipherable as something more than an array of problems to be fixed...there are deep and irremediable difficulties inherent in the liminal space traversed by student-teachers *that cannot and should not be fixed.* (1994b, 17)

The work of Felman (1987), Britzman and Pitt (1996), and Britzman (1998) would further suggest that the "problems" encountered in the liminal space are, in fact, what we need to become most curious about in our research. Interesting to note, too, how, as researchers, we are always, as Michelle Fine states, "implicated at the hyphen" (1994, 70). She is referring, of course, to the *other* hyphen—the "Self-Other hyphen" (70)—a tangled space in which we often write about others, forgetting to implicate our selves (as others) in the tangle. Perhaps a reading of the work of Fine, alongside that of Britzman and Jardine, is a tangled reminder that there are also deep and irremediable difficulties inherent in the liminal space traversed by Self-Other that cannot and should not be fixed. As Fine offers,

Our work will never
'arrive' but must
always struggle   'between'...(1994, 75).

My continued interest in the metaphor of a continual dawning, then, is for the ways it tangles metaphor, mixes metaphor. Melds. Dis-orients. Perhaps, a continual dawning might help us create new conditions of learning (to research) that would enable us to see our selves *differently* through this half-light and, in turn, to discover the ways that we ourselves are made different through the "light" of our research. A consideration of time as a continual dawning, then, is not only "about" becoming curious about the kinds of conditions that might enable us to conceptualize and enact the complexities of teaching and learning—events that we strive to somehow make visible—but also for how we might paint pictures of that pedagogy in an act of seeing—in a language—that allows and accounts for the repetition of unrepeatable acts. Perhaps, a time of continual dawning is itself curious—curiously tangled—in ways that remind us to question our seeing, a questioning that makes further (kinds of) (questions of our) "seeing" (im)possible.

To cure away ambivalence removes the eye with which we can perceive…the paradoxes of knowing and not-knowing…

The curricular claim for ambiguity as an important interpretive consideration is, therefore, at once pedagogical as well as methodological.

My continued interest in this chapter is to point to how, in the work of teacher education, our sense of time itself seems to call for "a new theory of time" (Lightman 1993). Following Deborah Britzman (1998), I am interested in
the act of becoming curious
of time—of turning time
into a curiosity.
"The curious time.
Of   [researching]   pedagogy."

For me, becoming curious about the curious time of researching pedagogy means imagining both in im/possible kinds of ways, keeping Milan Kundera's double-edged declarative in mind,

> Imagine a castle so big that it can't all be seen at once. Imagine a quartet that goes on for nine hours. There are anthropological limits—the limits of memory, for instance—that ought not to be exceeded. (Kundera 1986, 71)

Kundera, if we read him alongside Hélène Cixous, invites us to *try to paint what we cannot paint…to write what we cannot write before we have written*, to imagine becoming curious about the possibility of imagining the impossible. There are limits, of course, but writing is what you cannot know before you have written…and…imagining is what you cannot know before you have imagined it…and…researching is what you cannot know until you have researched it—until you have imagined researching/writing it. This is not to suggest that research is an imagining necessarily but, rather, that research is itself imaginative. Reading Shoshana Felman alongside Cixous and Kundera, we might say that "the lesson to be learned about [researching] pedagogy from [imagination] is less that of 'the application of [imagination] to pedagogy' than that of the implication of [imagination] in pedagogy and of pedagogy in [imagination]" (Felman 1987, 75). Kundera's invitation to imagine "a castle so big that it can't all be seen at once" is a curious invitation into interpretation, one that is inherently creative and one that is, in turn, hermeneutic, literary, pedagogic, and psychoanalytic, since all of these—through the tangle—are concerned "not just with what [imagination] says about teachers but with [imagination] itself as teacher" (Felman 1987, 75).

In this way, Kundera's essays on the rich dilemmas of working with/in words in *The Art of the Novel*, might also be read as *The Art of Research*. (Significant, too, that Kundera calls this particular set of essays of his "a practitioner's confession.") Through the tangle, then, a reading of Kundera's reading of the novel can also open out into possibilities for a generous reading of research.

> I've heard the history of [research] compared to a seam of coal long since exhausted. But isn't it more like a cemetery of missed opportunities, of unheard appeals? There are four appeals to which I am especially responsive...*The appeal of play*...*The appeal of dream*...*The appeal of thought*...[and] *The appeal of time*...(Kundera 1986, 15–16)

Bringing imagination to bear upon our acts of research and becoming curious about research as an imaginative act are reminders that our acts of research are themselves acts of reading and writing. Research is *performed* through acts of reading and writing that often become invisible through the tangle. Of course we must read and write to "produce" research, but, in this case, I am suggesting reading and writing "of a different order," a reading and a writing in which we, ourselves, must become implicated. That is, the nature of our research as a performative act can become increasingly available to us—more visible and potentially more profound in the ways it implicates us.

In my case, the experience of researching an experience of the practice of writing became most instructive when the research began to break down in a way that offered insight into a reading of my own experience of researching. A reading in which the question, "What is the experience of living a life that includes the practice of writing," could be read differently each time, through the tangle, as if for the first time. An ongoing reading in which my awareness of my practice of researching as a tangled form of reading and writing—of wordplay—became increasingly available to me, so that researching the tangle was, in a more literal sense, a reading and writing (of) the tangle. Researching writing. Writing research.

Becoming implicated in my own learning, in my own research of learning and teaching as acts of learning to read and write my own research differently has not only involved learning about the tangle, but learning from my experience in the tangle. Giving myself to the tangle—of learning to learnwriteteach...of learning to learnwriteresearch...of researching to learnreadwriteresearch —meant everything becoming seriously tangled, yet still recognizable in playful ways. Like Calvin, of *Calvin and Hobbes* fame, who, in one particular cartoon, finds himself deep in the tangle. In the opening frame of this particular strip, Calvin's world, in particular his bedroom, splinters into unrecognizable fragments as he begins to experience a radical and uncomfortable transformation which prompts an always classic Calvin monologue:

> *Calvin*: Oh No! Everything has suddenly turned neo-cubist! [tangled!] It all started when Calvin engaged his Dad in a minor debate! Soon Calvin could see both sides of the issue! Then poor Calvin began to see both sides of everything! The traditional single viewpoint has been abandoned! Perspective has been fractured! The multiple views provide too much information! It's impossible to move! Calvin quickly tries to eliminate all but one perspective...It works! The world falls into a recognizable order! [At which point Calvin returns to the living room and the scene of the argument with his father only to say] You're still wrong, Dad. (Watterson 1988, 120)

Unlike Calvin, my writing and researching—this particular sketch of a particular sketch—do not resolve quite as easily. And while becoming paralyzed by the tangle might become problematic, there is much to learn from living/writing/researching in the tangle, perhaps best represented by the hyphenated space of dis-comfort: somewhere in between comfortable and uncomfortable. Somewhere in between reading and writing and researching. Somewhere in between.

The cartoon of Calvin's dilemma is, in its own way, helpful for learning to become curious about this in-between time, about the curious time of researching pedagogy—the curious sense of time travel required to live and write and research, in between. For Calvin, time travel is frame-to-frame, though the cartoon strip can offer a writerly text that invites us to write (our own sense of) time into our reading. The cartoon invites us to imagine time, differently.

Kundera might call this "the appeal of time" in his reading of the experience of writing a novel. The tangle, in turn, works to show how the experience of reading a novel is also a form of writing and researching our experience of reading—a novel *or* research—and how our choosing to write time as an experience of reading, or to read time as an experience of writing, are influenced and made different by our naming of text as novel, or as research.

Kundera says, "the period of *terminal paradoxes* incites the novelist to broaden the time issue beyond the...problem of personal memory to the enigma of collective time" (1986, 16). He then offers ways for the writer and reader to begin to bend time, to make time malleable, to make time into a curiosity. He offers ways to *make* time. For the researcher to work in similar ways might mean creating new conditions of research that would enable both researcher and reader to be disturbed by time. To imagine time. To *make* time, differently. Through the tangle. Inciting the researcher to broaden the time issue beyond the problem of personal memory to the enigma of collective time means asking time to tangle. It means making certain demands on time, as well as certain demands on the ways we read and write and research time. It certainly demands that we begin to let go of our more traditional, literal, and linear conceptions of time.

This might mean, for example, framing time in curious ways that don't necessarily move us (or it) from frame to frame. It might mean writing research through a lens that, like *The Powers of Ten* film, moves us in ways beyond our imagining. If we were to move outward far enough to see our research framed from outer space, would it still be tangled? Or, in more conventional framings that still somehow become invisible as we read and write and research the tangle, how do we move—without becoming tangled—beyond our own personal memory of a (particular) classroom scene, to the time of teacher education in the early years of the twenty-first century? How do we conduct research without imposing a beginning or an end? What kinds of research become possible by a purposeful losing track of time (a becoming lost in order to be found, differently).

Might we also read/write other time signatures into our research in order to acknowledge the complex layerings of time that work with and against our particular work? We might, for example, read/write the textual representations of the media into the tangle (which are always and already part of the tangle even though we might not make them visible in our research). A reading of a prominent national newspaper at the time of this writing, for example, situates "the classroom," moving with and against a growing tangle of pedagogical relations. An education reporter whose words are written on a particular day for a particular deadline tells us that the provincial government's latest curriculum reform effort promises parents a solid school program that will provide knowledge and skills to compete and succeed in today's global economy.

It is significant to note that time has continued to stretch and pull me away from the "original" classroom experience in which my research interests lie: I have since travelled over 2,000 miles from that classroom at the edge of the Pacific Ocean to live in a small village perched above one of the Great Lakes, where I continue to write and live a pedagogy still brushed by coastal wind and salt water. The thin line that connects these dots, East and West, is subject to the vagaries of memory, geography, imagination, and grammar.

This particular tangle, then, becomes situated in a nest of particulars. A classroom of teacher candidates in Vancouver, British Columbia, has drifted east over the Rockies. Suffering from altitude sickness or perhaps just weary from travel, the prairies in between offer little preparation and certainly no innoculation for the kind of cynicism that a reading of "knowledge and skills to compete in the global economy" offers to my writing of the classrooms that I am currently living in. See how the classroom is the same everywhere? Different, too. See how tangled it gets? The tangled relations. But that's what happens when you follow Kundera's line in a way that Natalie Goldberg might have strung it. Like this line for example: "You have to let writing eat your life and follow it where it takes you. You fit into it; it doesn't fit neatly into your life" (Goldberg 1990, 156). And then Karen Connelly reappears...

This is where you are now. Then you turn your head away and you are somewhere else. The only truth is that there is none: Of course I have already written Karen Connelly so (in)visibly into the text, written Connelly so tightly into the script that she simply became italicized with no other mention of a source or a citation. Just: *watch in amazement. The thud of your bones. Realize what you've seen. Colliding. With the grace of birds.* Then looking back toward History, to John Dewey or Hannah Arendt and a playful collision of time and titles: "Art as the Life of the Mind." To Virginia Woolf or Lewis Carroll: "A Room with a View Through the Looking Glass." Or stretching forward to Graeme Gibson or Donna Haraway: "A Cyborg's Virtual Manifesto."

The time of research is a time for becoming curious about time. A time for becoming implicated in the ways we have learned to tell time—as though it were seamless. A time for becoming implicated in the ways we have learned to "write research" that is seemingly seamless; for creating texts which appear to "tell time" as it "really" is, as it "really" was. Creating a *researcherly* text, on the other hand, implicates us in the seams; it demands a reading/writing that acknowledges the gaps and fissures where time bends and folds. A researcherly text is curious about itself, as language, which is inextricably tied up with time. In our curricular travels, language becomes a way of marking time, of testing time, of wondering and worrying over time. Mindful always of the ambivalent sense of language itself: of possibility and constraint. As the poet Anne Michaels offers:

> Language is artificial of course, relying on juxtaposition to represent the world, just as the artist draws the imaginary line around the apple to create the illusion of its shape, to give the illusion of its depth. (1995, 180)

My continued interest in researching teachers' writing lives is very much tied to time travel and how we choose to navigate the course of time—in teacher education time and in the greater collective sense of time—our lifetime(s) lived as teachers and learners. In particular, I am interested in the conditions that might enable us to spend time together imaginatively in ways that both honor as well as disrupt time and our research of time spent in classrooms. Becoming self-conscious always of the illusions we create to give our (research of) pedagogy shape, depth, texture. Text-ure.

In our teaching, and in our research of teaching, wordmaking offers such possibilities. Words can act as timekeepers. Words can tell time. With words we can imagine time, even play with time, as Kundera does so beautifully in his writing. Is there a place in the research of teacher education for wordmaking? For wordplay? A place to fictionalize time? Poeticize time? Dream time? As I continue to remain curious about the curious time of pedagogy, I feel these kinds of questions are, in fact, worthy of our time in teacher education. When I have tried to write time into being, tried to imagine the time of pedagogy—of teacher candidates in writing workshops, the results have often taken me in directions I might never have imagined. Through the tangle, wordplay becomes (a form of) research. Research becomes (a form of) wordplay. *Research is itself wordplay.* Tangled. Imagine: a castle so big that it can't all be seen at once...Imagine: teacher education. Imagine: research.

Alan Lightman (1993) offers a provocative reading of time imagined differently as he ponders and plays with words, and with time in his novel *Einstein's Dreams*. He tangles time, sometimes hopefully, other times hopelessly. His novel's plot line is sometimes unrecognizable, at least in the ways we have come to recognize plot. Lines tangle round the plot, through the plot. Re-plotting time. Re-visiting time. Reinventing plot. Reimagining time. Tangling lines and lives. Like Karen Connelly's "Bowl of Yellow Flowers." Like wildmind writing. Like the "Small Imaginings" (in chapter 2). Like research.

In these ways, Lightman's writings make for interesting curricular imaginings—of time, of research, of lines and lives. His textual wordplay offers a location for becoming curious about researching pedagogy:

In this world, there are two times. There is mechanical time and there is body time. The first is as rigid and metallic as a massive pendulum or iron that swings back and forth, back and forth, back and forth. The second squirms and wriggles like a bluefish in a bay. The first is unyielding, predetermined. The second makes up its mind as it goes along. (23)

And while it would be unfair and stereotypical to think of curricular time, and much of our research of the curious time of pedagogy as mechanical time, school time, it takes little imagination to put ourselves in that place. Back and forth. Back and forth. The curious time of researching pedagogy, as I am beginning to imagine it, however, squirms and wriggles...makes up its mind as it goes along.

Continual dawning. Iron pendulum. Bluefish. A bowl of yellow flowers. All hold possibility for imagining the curious time of pedagogy. Of significance to this particular imagining are the ways that time bends and folds in upon itself, collides and clashes in ways that speak to the difficulty of learning (to tell time).

In the case of my research work with teacher candidates, time colors my attempt to hold time long enough to dwell with a particular set of lived experiences and, in turn, to provide some kind of picture of that seeing. Lost with/in time, I am often left, simply, imagining—"caressing each moment as an emerald on temporary consignment" (Lightman 1993, 9).

Linear time asked that I proceed outwards from the "Small Imaginings" that appeared in chapter 2, add flesh to the characters and dimensionality to their living in a narrative we might come to recognize in some way, possibly even as our own. (The Small Imaginings, as you may recall, were my initial attempts at re-presenting my experience of spending time with a particular group of preservice teachers.) At the time, these Imaginings offered a way to give tentative shape to a particular experience, to which I hoped to give further shape. Calling them "Imaginings" was my own self-reflexive strategy for bringing into question their "realness." Though I employed certain textual strategies that invited (a) certain kind(s) of reading(s), there was still a sense in which day had to follow night—the imaginings had to be made (more) real. Even if, as Linda Hutcheon has offered, we are invited to read the text as a "likely story" where language and convention and meaning become slippery surfaces, it seems there must still be enough textual placeholders to attend to the characters that move between the classroom and *the road that curves around the wet blue belly of the sea.* Yet, it seems we learn to trust our sense of balance only as we become un/comfortable with our footing.

With the curious time of research *making up its mind as it went along*, I chose to entertain the possibility of a textual location that might create new conditions for (learning to) research. Without knowing what I was doing (because there is never a full coincidence between practice and awareness), I attempted to enact a research involving writing practice, using wordplay as a way of becoming curious, not only about the research of writing, but also the experience of writing research. *Writing* research. Wordplay seemed to offer a way to begin to address and entertain the tangle. In a sense, chapter 2, "A Bowl of Yellow Flowers," *became* the research just as the research became a bowl of yellow flowers. Was this merely a short form? Of fiction? Of research? Was I simply imagining this being research? Imagining this as a form of research? Was I simply imagining research in a manner that might best be described as fictional research? Or, researcherly fiction?

For me, the time of research became a time of tangle. A tangling. At the risk of mixing metaphors, each new foothold was a reminder of how tenuous the footing was becoming. Yet, as I became steeped in the work of other writers and researchers who spoke of bending and folding and otherwise disrupting linear time, it became more and more possible to consider using footholds to take flight.

I continued to be both blessed and cursed by the "symptoms" of the lived experience of a discovery as Felman talked about it: Breakthroughs. Leaps. Discontinuities. Regressions. Deferred actions. *Like a blue fish in a bay, time squirmed and wriggled.* The following passage, a journal entry that mapped my ongoing process at the time, captures some of the ways that the tangle became pedagogical...

> Neither day nor night. This is the point where I
> am beginning to question, among many things,
> my footing. I wonder, "Do the Small Imagin-
> ings grow larger or smaller, more or less real, as

I continue to move forward and backward through my (re)searchings?" Certainly, my expectations were that the imaginings would grow—and they have—but I now seem unprepared for the possibility that growth would take them in a direction that might disrupt my "findings." That is, my ability or perhaps more accurately, my desire to stretch these imaginings on to a template (of time)—a timeplate?—that might be more recognizable/ acceptable, more real, within the scholarly discourse of which I seek to be a part now seems lacking. I seem to know less and less about what "actually" took place during my lived experience in the shared space of a particular classroom—now long gone—at a time when I (am) expect(ed) to know more and more. And, strange—or maybe not—I desire less and less to say what may have happened and want, simply, to imagine what I would like to (have seen)/see happen. Daignault's earlier comments continue to circulate and inform my writing and thinking: sometimes our research is "too real." What theory of time might honor this kind of (re)search?

Perhaps this is all an elaborate way of saying that this is as good as it gets. The small imaginings are just what they are. Small. Imaginings. And given the choice, I would prefer to create a curricular form that might allow me/us to remain in a place where these imaginings, these images, are left to linger as sub/textual fragments that haunt and inform my research without (certain kinds of) explanation. Or, perhaps—and I am hopeful here—this is the beginnings of (imagining) a "new" theory of time for educational research, one that, like teaching and learning, needs to account for the sense of terminal vertigo one tends to experience in attempting to live well with the tangle of research over extended periods of time. A time that repeats itself, a time that moves backwards and forwards, a time that is directionless, a time that does not recognize itself. As Alan Lightman offers,

> Imagine a world
> in which there is no time. Only
> images...footprints
> in the snow on a winter island...
> dust on the window sill...the eye
> of a needle...a child on a bicycle...smiling
> the smile of a lifetime...a worn book lying
> on a table beside a dim lamp. (Lightman 1993, 75–79) [1]

Four chapters, seven interludes, and one preface later, I remain curious about the curious time of researching pedagogy. Lightman's imaginings—"a world in which there is no time...only images"—continue to hold up a fascinating, if slightly distorted, mirror whose reflections offer other interesting interpretive possibilities for imagining the curious time of researching pedagogy. While Lightman's text identifies itself as fiction, my reading of it with and against other kinds of research(erly fiction), as well as other kinds of fiction(al research) create the possibility of a more ambivalent reading of both fiction *and* research where *identity is itself fictional.* [It seems I am (still) learning to read/write/read research *differently.*]

The negotiation of textual identity continued to tangle in and across an already tangled liminal space in which the acts of learning and teaching, researching and writing began to bleed into one another, leaving a water-colored world that offered itself to interpretation in a Rorschach-styled reading.

Mary Aswell Doll (1995, 130–132) asks, "How might we read [such a] world? Read our selves?" She responds to her own query by suggesting that we might learn to read "with an eye far behind the 'I'...we must revalue objects; we must become less literal; we must devalue clock time." And my response to Mary Aswell Doll?

---

[1] I have taken the liberty of "poeticizing" these images from Lightman's prose, rearranging them into different lines and shapes on the page.

cLocK tImE: a WaY oF uN/kNoWiNg

Can you imagine no
time in schools? No time
pieces to measure a day's worth:
how many minutes left in Language
Arts   how long   'til lunch...Imagine
instead a blank space on the wall—a perfectly empty
circle that does not return our watch-full stares,
refuses to confirm our constant glancings wall-ward.
No glass face to mirror our selves in time or
show us our selves being
on time   in time   late...

...Do you remember the classroom?
How time used to freeze
just before the minute-hand convinced
the hour-hand it was time
to move: Every hour on the hour. And every eye
turned too.   The clock's face...
Entire school districts lost in that tiny window
of time tripping over itself in tune to the buzzing
sound the clock made straining under
so much   pressure   to tell time
and then the release
to know ourselves timeless again
time forgotten...Can you re-member

The moment? when
the cardboard clock with the move-able hands stopped
playing games and simply created its own
shiny curriculum out of the reach
of hands that wished otherwise? And who would dare build
a house-of-cards, chair-on-desk-ladder up to time
to turn the tiny cog on Mr. Henderson's clock and trick time
into thinking
that history (period 7) was over? (With thirty minutes to
spare.)
Trying to trick the teacher into thinking

time was up…How many years

later? Back in school to become
a teacher. Who would have thought
you'd find yourself trying to trick time again
the curious time of pedagogy, no time pieces to measure
how time is going…the Shiny Curriculum.
Who would dare build a blank space,
the tiny cog tripping perfectly
a glass face   straining.
No time in schools. And every eye turned
too.

Can you imagine teachers (s)training
under the pressure to tell time? You need
some way to talk about their telling
of time. So you move
the hands yourself, build
a cardboard clock to freeze the perfect
ladder up to the curious space.
Watch-full. Waiting. No simple measure
to read time's worth. Every Our on the
hour.

I offer "Clock Time" as a whimsical poem, curricular or
otherwise, for the ways that words sometimes fall out as play in
the midst of "serious" work, and for how words sometimes point
to possibilities beyond the literal if we allow them to. Wordplay:
this is part of the invitation to think differently about preservice
teachers thinking differently about their time together in
classrooms. Thinking differently about time. Writing. Imagining.
*Can the study of the self studying education create new conditions of
researching and the making of pedagogical insight?* As poet Anne
Michaels suggests, "time enters language in many ways" (1995,
179). I believe that wordplay "knows" differently; in turn, it
invites us to interpret our Selves and our relations differently. Our
knowing and our meaning making—made possible through our
relationships with and through words—are influenced by our
work and play with text. The "simple" act of moving words

around the page alters the ways we (get to) know text, the ways we get to know knowing. Turning our own learning into a curiosity. Turning our researching of our learning. Into a curiosity.

Can prose become
poetry simply
by bending
or straightening
lines so that the words fly
down from their delicate perches
and fall into new
configurations?

Can the different ways
we line our world
also give shape to the ways we live
our lives?

Can wordplay enable us to become curious about the bending
and straightening of both lines and lives,
so that thinking about our work with beginning teachers is a
becoming curious
about the *shift from a preoccupation with researching the learning
of others*
to a consideration of the conditions for one's own learning to
research
(the learning of others)
(researching)...

The closest I have come to imagining these kinds of conditions, ones that might best support and sustain, and suspend, the curious time of researching pedagogy occur in my encounters with researcherly texts that offer opportunities, as David Jardine describes them, to

write and research differently...
about the life of our children, our schools, the life
of mathematics or the intricate
meaty heart of science, or the curves
and contours of reading and writing [which] require

dwelling in language that can itself hold life
in its sway, beyond the clear and simple
and harsh namings requisite of [so much of our] research. (Rasberry and
Jardine 1995, 1)

Loosening the hold of literalism that underwrites much of educational discourse, "we find ourselves in a different space, where the unfamiliar beckons because it resists labels...It is wondrous to be among unfamiliarity" (Doll 1995, 129). At the risk of losing track of curricular time, I would like to conjecture that becoming curious about the nature of time in our work in and out of classrooms—(the) time(s) that "contain little moments, very little moments, which allow us to turn our attention" (Doll 1995, 143)—might help us to begin to imagine writing research differently. Unearthing some of the ways we dwell with words—the attention turned toward cadence and breath, connection and disconnection, obsession, text/uality, method and unmethod, space and location, construction and expression, deconstruction, non/sense, play and work, literary infusions, form and mystery, imagination, commitment, dis/belief, knowing and not knowing—point toward a poetics of educational research and a way to begin to dwell with pedagogy; that is, a way of playing with meaning(s), and with words that enable us to *make* research...

...It's about how we interact
with texts like poems that show us ourselves
in important ways   and complicate
our learning. It's not learning
about poetry as research or research as poetry,
but learning *from* our experience of writing
poetry as research and research as poetry,
as we choose to play with the naming of them.
It's the possibility that our learning to read certain kinds of
writing as research, certain kinds of research
as writing might offer insight into the making of
insight which is itself a condition for discovering
our selves as researchers researching
our selves through others,
as others

as other...

At the heart of this "new" theory of time in teacher education "lies the seemingly paradoxical assumption that learning how one learns from the lives, histories, cultures, and dilemmas of others involves a close study of one's own conditions of learning" (Britzman and Pitt 1996, 119).

...."All that we need
to decide, each day, when the light
is right, is where and when
to draw the   line"...Returning to Grumet's

words, I am suggesting that thinking
about poetry and research—poetry as research and
research as poetry—and how both, as wordplay, offer ways to
pay attention, ways

to attend to the work and (word)play of teaching and learning
under the uncertain and often unsteady light
that attention draws into form(s) that (in turn) draw
our attention. It provides us with ways to draw

the line, knowing and not knowing
that the light may never be
"right."

                              * * *

Here we are, los domingueros, the Sunday people, drunk to exhaustion with light and the dusty scent of African wind. The bright blue benches behind me are soft with the bodies of old people, tense with the knuckles and knees of young lovers. The old people wait patiently for the farther darkness, the young for the closer one.

A time of continual dawning blurs the boundaries between question and answer, between teaching and learning, between one story and another, between self and other. The light goes on and on with little opportunity to stop time or ask for directions.

From here, it looks clean, children tumbling playfully, doll-limbed, the people (featureless, really, at this distance) fine and strong, leaving well-formed footprints behind them.
Karen Connelly's poetic images inadvertently characterize some of the ways in which we so often come to recognize our selves in our research, our small imaginings: *from here it looks clean*...In my case, the light of my imaginings, along with the images that Karen Connelly has painted from atop the broad stone wall which, like poetry, continue to create/capture just enough light for an interpretive location that enables me/us to appreciate their complexity, question their existence, and puzzle over the relations that st(r)ain the canvas. But the light also creates its own conditions, sets other interpretive movements into play. Neither day nor night. As the storyline would have us believe, the characters leave well-formed footprints behind them. Yet just as I observe Connelly observing her characters from the wall—*The old people are gazing at the cliffs, ignoring the white threads of cataracts, seeing perfectly the greenness of other lives, other decades, thinking of the ancient lime trees towering beyond them.* I also observe myself observing the realness of her fiction. And the fiction of her realness. What do *these* observations announce? Her writerly text invites my reading it, writing it in ways that move with and against the seeing. I am sometimes satisfied to let Connelly tell me what the old people are seeing just as I am sometimes resistant to her omniscient "I." She can't know what they're seeing. In turn, my "researcherly" text provides an invitation to interpretation-made-more-visible, as well as more question-able; it offers ways to become curious about time, both in learning to teach and in learning to talk/write about time from the middle of the tangle; it is an invitation to consider how we are made different through the relations that researchly texts make available. Researchly texts offer ways to address these kinds of issues by inviting us to become curious about our own learning, our own writing, our own researching. Researchly texts create new conditions of learning that enable the making of insight, the ability to discover what it is we are learning, writing, researching, through a reading of our own experience of researching.

I am only now discovering, through the tangle, why "A Bowl of Yellow Flowers" has been so important without necessarily knowing why: Connelly's story as writerly text is a piece of fictional research, while mine is a piece of researcherly fiction. The tangle is fiction/al. (The) fiction is tangled...

The wall is low: I sit on its back, watching the way the morning light washes the letters off the board: Invisible pedagogy...The B.Ed. students from the tech studies program slump in the last row of the classroom hoping that language cannot traverse the great curricular distance from front to back. Physics students perform routine calculations that might provide at least temporary immunity to poetry. History majors count on their subject discipline to repeat itself. English teachers-to-be gloat or glow in their seats. The instructor shouts language across the curriculum...A girl with hair the color of clean straw is staring at her watch, desperate for time to slide open...I wonder if I am imagining it all...

    I can't know what they are   seeing,
    through the tangle   the fonts melt
    and mingle.
           Italics can no longer be counted
    on. Here is a broad stone   wall.

    Yes, it's just as Winterson describes:
    in the moment of passing,
    the canvas has more power to stop me than I have power
    to walk   on.

waiting for our names to be called

_____ INTERLUDE

"three stabs at poetry"[2]

My first memory of "creative" writing was grade nine. I attended a boarding school which was run in the old English tradition. I remember that every Tuesday we were told to write a 200-word essay on a common subject. A week later, we read our textbooks in class while we waited for our names to be called. We then walked up to the teacher's desk and gave him our work. We stood by his desk as he read the essay...

1.
Fresh out of school, Indian and Native Affairs employed me
to visit native Indian bands across the province.
I was to instruct them:
How to maintain their sewers and water systems.

Rather arrogant engineers had told me stories
of being chased off the land by gun-toting natives.
They were glad to no longer work with any lazy Indians.

For a year I traveled between reserves—
some in the city, others isolated
by uneasy hours in float planes.

They would test you, I found out.
My car was in the Chief's spot (the gravel lot was enormous)
or I was too young—there must be some mistake.
All with faces like stone.
But with poorly disguised humor in their eyes.

The Chief would eventually greet me at the band office.
"Let's go for a drive." No explanation.
"Engineer, huh? You married? Why are you doing this?"

---

[2] This is an excerpt of one preservice teacher's "literacy narrative" written in class, along with a trio of his poems—"first evers"—written some weeks later. I have taken the liberty of italicizing his literacy narrative excerpts and juxtaposing them with his poetry.

Slow down

I met kind grandmothers who served up fresh prawns
while the men searched for someone lost at sea.
Pipelayers who laughed like kids at my fear of slugs.
Chiefs who shared salmon sandwiches
and pointed to where someone's son had jumped off the water
tower.

Half pace. No bonuses here.
The project manager would come by and demand
"What the hell's been going on here?"
I too wanted to chase him away.

*Sometimes our writing was met with approval and our teacher read out
some paragraphs to the class. Some work was also substandard and was
read out to the class as well. My work was read aloud often as I was still
learning to master the English language. Knowing that there was a good
chance for public embarrassment, my friends and I wrote safely—simple
sentences with verbs and punctuation we knew how to handle...*

2.
I held an engineering job once, for three years. A productive
company.

We had no lunchroom, no couch or soft seats to gather at.
We would roll up our blueprints and eat our sandwiches
At the drafting tables.
There was no lunch hour—people ate at different times and
took as long
As they thought necessary, or appropriate.
Conversation between the desks would shift between work
and golf.

Around my first Christmas there, memos were sent out;
We could request any capital expenditures from the company.

The couch which I asked for never materialized, of course. Others
Had requested new drafting pens and tape measures.
I felt like an idiot. Besides, there was no room for a sitting area.

I began to drive to Burnaby Lake and eat lunch in the bird sanctuary.
A draftsman asked me with a wink where I was off to every day.
I shouldn't have said that I was having lunch with the ducks.

What a rich symbol a couch would have provided us!
You deserve a rest.
Get comfortable and talk about your family or your weekend.
Sure, we can fit three on here!
As it was, we often ate our lunches in silence, separated
By drafting tables and walls of design manuals.

We could have crossed the floor, of course, and joined
Someone at their desk, or sat on the grass outside.
But for the same reason that I felt like a fool for having eaten
with the ducks, we never did.

Although our year in grade nine English killed
our creativity and courage to explore
the possibilities of language, we did become
precise and grammatically sound
writers...

3.
I walked to school in the wintertime.

Dawn would be hours away.
I would imagine that I was the only one awake,
As I crunched my way through the snow.

You could let your eyelashes meet and the street lights
Would disappear into pinpricks surrounded by dim halos.
I would see how long I could stay in this fantastical landscape
Until a snowbank would nudge me along the path again.

On cold mornings, your breath would be left behind in a trail
of puffs.
The snow could shatter like breaking glass.
Chunks of it would be booted along for a while.

Those days there were two types of darkness.

There was the kind that filled the basement hallway
As you fumbled frantically for the light switch at the far end.
It would let you sleep only when the door was cracked
And a pen knife was unfolded in the dresser.

But there was also the peaceful emptiness
That was company in the mornings.
No shapeless evildoers sizing you up from behind.
Just a delightful silence. A vast black slate waiting
For a child's imagination; fields of snow crystals
Brought to life by a porchlight,
Huge white mushrooms instead of mailboxes.
A gentle and dreamlike introduction to the day.

trust me I'm (almost) a doctor:
poetry and pedagogy and teachers
writing lives

_____ INTERLUDE

I. "Listening into a Cadence"

The Canadian poet Dennis Lee offers these powerful words that speak of/to the fragile conditions that connect the writer and the writing, the poet and the poem, the re-searcher and the search:

> Most of my time as a poet is spent listening into a luminous tumble, a sort of taut cascade. I call it "cadence." If I withdraw from immediate contact with things around me, I can sense it churning, flickering, thrumming, locating things in more shapely relation to one another. (1998, 3)

From the middle, end, beginning of my re-search—from somewhere between the known and the not known—comes a poem: "Trust Me I'm (Almost) a Doctor—Poetry and Pedagogy and Teachers Writing Lives." The lines of this particular poem grew out of my earliest experiences as a doctoral student working with a group of preservice teachers "work-shopping" across the curriculum. (This involvement would mark the beginnings of my fascination with the ways that a classroom full of preservice teachers embraced writing practice on the way to teaching.) I have been living (with) this poem for quite some time now, workshopping it endlessly in the hopes of finding "dazzlement," Kundera's wonderful word for "the truth *to be discovered*" (1986, 117). (A poet who serves any other kind of truth, according to Kundera, is a "false poet.") Kundera's emphasis on the "to-be-discovered" nature of truth is, for me, an affirmation of the need to learn to live well with the indeterminacy that is always and already part of our poetry and our pedagogy—and of our living. Truth, then, like knowledge, "is not a cognitive possession. It is an event: the singular event of a discovery…[that]…has to be repeated, reenacted, practised each time for the first time" (Felman 1987, 12). So each reading of my poem, each revisit, is a re-verb-eration in the way that we might coin new verbs from existing nouns—a "shift from the done to the doing…an enacting (not an enactment)" (Davis 1996, xv).

I resonate strongly with the intimate details of Dennis Lee's own workings with words—of his asking words to perform the unimaginable: to mean. And to breathe. Life. All the while performing the contagious and contradictory act of attempting to write about the presence of an experience by cutting oneself off from that source. Lee continues:

> More and more I sense this cadence as presence—though it may take 50 or 100 revisions before a poem enacts it—I sense it as presence, both outside myself and inside my body opening out and trying to get into words. What is it?...

> But the cadence of the poems I have written is such a small and often mangled fraction of what I hear, it tunes out so many wavelengths of that massive, infinitely fragile polyphony, that I frequently despair. And often it feels perverse to ask what is cadence, when it is all I can manage to heed it...

> You heard an energy, and those lives were part of it. Under the surface alienation and the second-level blur of words there was a living barrage of meaning: private, civil, religious—unclassifiable finally, but there, and seamless, and pressing to be spoken. And I felt that press of meaning: I had no idea what it was, but I could feel it teeming toward words. I called it cadence...And hearing that cadence, I started to write again. (Lee 1995, 397–401)

In "listening in to cadence," the closeness of my poem and those lives who were a part of it—its presence—is most strongly felt in its absence, the distance that grows wild between the lines and the lives that helped to grow the poem in the first place. As Madeleine Grumet, in her poignant description of our work as teachers and researchers, states, "So it is the shadow of the experience of teaching that we pursue here, hoping that we might catch a glimpse of its distortions and of the ground on which it falls..." (1988, 61). The farther away as you get closer, it would seem, eyes forever adjusting to the light. I offer a re-presentation of the poem in this interlude, not for the answers it might reveal but for the questions it helps me to continue living:

II. Trust Me I'm (Almost) a Doctor: Poetry and Pedagogy and Teachers Writing Lives (Rasberry 1994, 17–20).

Words spoken with
voices, polite and earnest:

"Excuse me, but how much will the final assignment be worth??"
and…
"How many words should that include??"
and…
"Should that be single or double-spaced??"
and…
"Can you tell us how it will be graded??"
and…
"Does punctuation count??"

Words unspoken with
voices, angry and confused and earnest:

"I've been burned too many times in other courses to trust this one nutty professor."
and…
"This creative stuff sounds good but I've got my grade point average to consider."
("Yeah, and what about jobs next year.")
and…
"Hey, I'm actually being asked to write what I really want to write."
and…
"This stuff is not going to go over too well in the school where I'm practice teaching."
and…
"Just give me the usual assignment please, tell me what to do, spell it out, I don't have time."

All these words spoken and
unspoken, tough to digest
hard to swallow

uttered and unuttered,
muttered
by soon-to-be TEACHERS
TEACHER candidates
those who would TEACH

fine honest intelligent
people   searching questioning
people   meaning-makers

an elite band of women and men
well-schooled
well-intentioned
well-off
well-educated
well-honed
well-meaning
well within the bell curve
well—what happened?

when these

teachers-to-be were offered a taste of freedom
a drink from the well
a shot in the arm
a chip off the old block
a bird in the hand,

an opportunity:

to take risks with their writing
to bungee jump with pen and paper
(see Jack) run and (see Jane) jump and (close both those books
and) play with language
to be playful in language
to slip and slide and
skip and skate
celebrate the
slipperiness

of language.

What happened?
when they were challenged

to construct
to deconstruct
fall down
get up again
fly
tune an ear to the slippery scales of discourse
to make a renewed commitment to their own writing
claim ownership
write and write and write and write:
personally creatively expressively.

What happened??
when they were given
a call to experiment without clinical details or
pre and post tests
no white lab coats
a chance
to acknowledge the value of expository essays but write a play
a poem a radio drama.

An invitation:

to build a campfire with words
explode sentences into brilliant flashes of fireworks
dig holes in the backyard and bury the bones of favorite lines
for
safekeeping,
for later discovery.

To spill and splash buckets of blue and yellow and purple ink
over familiar and not-so-familiar experiences (like learning
and teaching),
ride the rapids ski the slopes bag the peaks fly the sky,

an affable offer
to be reflective
to be self-reflexive
to be …

To discover that writing
   is like a love letter to the world
   is like walking on water
   is like waiting for the tide to come in
   is like pulling teeth.

To discover that writing
   is a sweat-stubbed pencil
   is the dust in your cuffs
   is water flowing uphill
   is heavenly
   is hellish
   is braving the visit.

To discover that writing is like scaling the outside
of a downtown office tower during rush hour:
alone   in a crowd.

To discover that writing is like being
given the first volume of a set of   Encyclopedia.

All these discoveries
but still,
an invitation for teacher candidates
   to live writerly lives
   to work with words
   to word their worlds
   sculpt their own stories
   rearrange their narratives
   write themselves into/out of existence.

An unlimited offer
for teacher candidates to take pen and paper and scratch
out a sermon

scribble a poem
shed tears over a story
exalt over an essay.

To discover
epistemological graffiti,
the anatomy of voice.

To shape polish and sculpt sentences
experiment with artifice
question coherence
engage in decorative doodling
try on new hats
throw off old clothes
swim in an ocean of signs and symbols and signifiers,

recognize that language is
everything
everywhere
a sea of   textuality.

Time to go for broke
time to get and give pleasure through
jotting
journalling
joking
jesting.

Well, WHAT HAPPENED?

Well, as you might
guess, the course was
exciting
invigorating
liberating
confusing
chaotic
troubling and
tricky—it was disturbing.

All of these students set free with pen and paper and nothing
but their lives to back them up:

some to float up into the giant steel blue sky in a colorful hail
of helium balloons (not particularly worried
about coming down)
some to waterski their way over blue-green lakes of glass
(at high speeds, breathless and waving through the wake)
some to ride slow and steady, John Deere-like, on backyard
tractors (self-mulching mowers moving

in carefully calculated circuits)
some to sink slowly in the brown and earthly
mud (up to the axles in self-discovery)
some to plunge headlong over cliffs
(and disappear at the bottom in a puff
of smoke like Wile E. Coyote)
and some to stop dead in their tracks
(rabbits frozen by the icy white highway stare of oncoming
headlights).

And many left to wonder:

WHAT HAPPENED??
and
WHEN do we get to do this kind of writing and living again?
and
WHY didn't this happen sooner?
and
WHERE does schooling end and life begin?
and
WHO was it that told me I couldn't write in the first place?
and
HOW do I help my own students to write personally and
expressively and creatively?
and
HOW will we be graded
on this assignment?

CHAPTER SIX

Teachers Writing Lives

> In writing, we can rest and float; move and yet not move. It shows us
> the patterns we are weaving with our lives; it can help us to make the
> patterns and to change the patterns all at once.
>
> —Cynthia Chambers, *Composition and Composure*, 1998.

What follows are the words of a teacher candidate written
sometime around the middle of the course; they are part of a
teacher's writing life, part of an unending process of a teacher
writing her life. There are only eighty-four words in this passage.
Not that many words with which to write a life, but they provide
a location from which to begin talking about writing. About
living. About teaching. About identity.

> Who do I want to be as a teacher? I want to be a facilitator of joy, a
> friend, a guide along the journey, an establisher of comfort. I want to be
> a source of reassurance, enthusiasm, and encouragement. I want to be a
> human being. I want to be like the girl with the flashlight who works in
> the planetarium as the star guide, pointing out constellations and
> planetary configurations in her beam. I want my students to see the
> universe of language. (*K.S.* May 1994)

The passage is polished. It is poetry. The words seems to catch
small pieces of sunlight in their turning. They reflect. They refract.
We are different for the light that passes through. The passage is
also pedagogy. The words begin to write a (teaching) life. Poetry
and pedagogy. Both are hope-full. Full of promise. The words
lead. Lead to other places in ways that open up possibilities for
living and teaching. The living leads. To words, to wordmaking
that makes other words possible. The words also mis-lead, as does
the living. They create a sense of unity and completeness, of
wholeness, even. As though the teaching life were (already)
written. So words also close down possibility. They constrain.

If we were to begin to "workshop" this teacher candidate's
piece of writing, which is also a piece of living, (the writing is
attached to a life being lived), we would be engaging in a

curricular act. One that is pedagogical at many levels. Within the space of the writing workshop—which in this case is also a place of teacher education—we might choose to establish the kinds of conditions on any given day that would enable us, as learners and teachers and writers, to engage with our writing and our words in different kinds of ways.

If, for example, we were to treat a particular class as a writing workshop in some of the ways that the writing workshop has been conceptualized, the primary focus would be on a work-shopping of our words—of our *lines*. We would be learners and writers (who also happen to be teachers) working with our words, working with our texts, engaged in various writerly acts (anything from writing process to copyediting). If, on the other hand, we were to treat a particular class as a "teacher education workshop," borrowing some of the writing workshop's pedagogical underpinnings, then the focus would lean toward a work-shopping of our words—of our *lives*. We would be learners and teachers (who also happen to be writers) working with our words, working with our texts, engaged in various teacherly acts (writing ourselves into real and imagined roles in classrooms and schools).

Of course, the question of whether it is, in fact, possible to make such neat and tidy distinctions in our writing and our living—between our lines and our lives—is itself open to question, is itself a deeply pedagogical question: when are our words simply words? What does it mean, in our textual living, to move a word, remove a word, suggest that a student, or a colleague, or a friend—or all of these combined—change a word in their writing? In the teacher candidate's passage of words above, for example, what might it mean to workshop her words, to work with "just" her words, just her "lines"? (As though it were poetry.) We might then begin to make editorial kinds of suggestions:

> I'm not sure about your choice of the word "friend" here; it doesn't seem to look right on the page...

> A line break after the "I want to be" might create an interesting effect. The reader might then receive an invitation

to read existentially: e.g., "I want to be," before the eye drops down to the next line "a teacher"...

I love the image of "pointing out constellations"! (Constellations and planetary configurations make a lovely sounding pair. What about arranging the words on the page to create some kind of night-skyed visual effect?)...

Why have you chosen to use the word "girl" here? At first it stopped me but now it really works...

That last line is beautiful: "I want my students to see the universe of language." (Wow.)

On the other hand, this same series of "editorial" questions and concerns might carry different meaning when they are directed toward her (teaching) life. (As if it were pedagogy.)

I'm not sure about your choice of the word "friend" here (what does it mean to call a teacher a friend? A friend a teacher?)...

I love the image of "pointing out constellations"! (In what ways are you pointing them out? Is it important to name the constellations? Do you leave room for the students to also point the constellations out to you?)...

That last line is beautiful: "I want my students to see the universe of language." (Wow.)

But when are we "just" work-shopping the lines, the writing that might be a poem or an essay or, in this case, the words that make up a deeply personal manifesto for a life that includes teaching? Can we ever act primarily as writers, who are also teachers, where the decision to change the word "girl" to "woman" or "whatever" might be based more on the way that it changes the look or "feel" of the sentence? And, when are we "just" work-shopping the lives, the living that goes on *in* the lines? (And in between the lines? Can we ever act primarily as teachers, who are also writers, where decisions to change words like "friend" to "partner" or "facilitator" to "mentor" or "counselor" or "co-learner" or "collaborator" or "teacher" might be based more on a pedagogical sensibility that bears philosophical and/or theoretical underpinnings about the nature of the teaching relationship than on the sounds and signs of poetry?

Either way, the manner in which we choose to work with words, our own and those with whom we learn and teach, is a highly charged and significant pedagogical act/ion. (How much more charged can it be when one person in a position of supposed authority suggests that another person, who has his or her own author-ity, make a change to a line? To a life?)

...In writing, we can rest and float; move and yet not move...

My interest, after spending a significant amount of time with teacher candidates engaged in curricular acts of writing and learning and teaching, is in conceptualizing the workshop as a location that is both a "work-shop," and a "word-shop." A place where we work with both lines *and* lives.

...It shows us the patterns we are weaving with our lives...

I have come to think of the ENED 426 experience as a place of "work-shopping," where "word-shopping"[1] takes place. The hyphen introduces a space for the lines and lives to come together and apart: We are our lines. We are not our lines. We are our lives. We are not our lives. Our lines are our lives. Our lines are not our lives. We are our words. We are not our words

---

[1] I have, with the help of other readers of this work, begun to use the term "word-shopping," to describe the work-shopping of words that took place within the language across the curriculum workshop. My initial use of the term "workshopping" was to emphasize the notion of teacher candidates trying the "work of teaching"—that is, the "job" called teacher—on for fit. Word-shopping, on the other hand, more closely describes the work of the writer or poet (and in our particular class the teacher) engaged in a form of writing practice which, in this case, deals explicitly with trying on (words which are intimately connected to) the practice of teaching. Thus, word-shopping holds the possibility of transcending an activity in a workshop as it becomes a life practice of trying on both lines *and* lives.

...it can help us to make the patterns and to change the patterns all at once...

My identity, my role, in re-presenting this particular teacher candidate's writing life, whose words form the opening passage in this chapter, as well as the particular group of teacher candidates whose writing lives inform this book, is not only that of researcher. I am also a poet, a writer, a teacher. I am drawn to words, to the lines *and* lives, in ways that sometimes seem to converge, other times seem to contradict. In each of these roles, however, I am seeking to engage with other human beings who are, in turn, engaged in acts of meaningmaking, most often through acts of wordmaking. My role—my identity—is an ambiguous one, both productive and precarious; it is in flux, as are the identities of the future teachers I have shared lines and lives with. We write the teaching life as it is written for us.

Work-shopping offers a place of both convergence and contradiction, a curricular location in which to practice word-shopping, a place to try on both lines and lives in a living that includes the practice of writing. And teaching. The workshop is, in this way, a collection of teachers' writing lives, just as it is a place where teachers collect and construct their lives.

Teachers' writing lives. Teachers writing (their) lives. This play on words is also the play of pedagogy, a pedagogy that attempts to "make space for students to *perform differently*". (Orner 1996, 77). The work-shop, then, offers a commonplace to entertain various and varying forms of identity negotiation through word-shopping.

In *Releasing the Imagination* Maxine Greene writes,

> Neither my self nor my narrative can have, therefore, a single strand. I stand at the crossing point of too many social and cultural forces; and in any case, I am forever on the way. (1995, 1)

Forever on the way. Yes. This seems an appropriate way to characterize ourselves as students of teacher education. Works-in-progress. In-process. Wanting. To know. In flux. Subject to entropy. Everything depending: Who are we? What names do we place on ourselves and our actions? Our complexities. Our identities. How could we? Should we? Ever? When, simply: it depends. Even so, we are required, for equally appropriate and necessary reasons, to forever stop and define ourselves, as teachers and learners—as human beings—who choose to do this rather than that, be here and not there. We wrestle with questions, always, of identity: needing one, not wanting others. Living with/in the familiar strangeness of identity's disciples of desire and curiosity and compulsion, of necessity and refusal and uncertainty. Living with/in the strange familiarity created by the tension between who we are and who we are not, who we want to be and who we may not want to become.

Identity is ambulatory, it moves as we move yet resists motion detectors. Caught up in the world of teaching and learning, we are swept along by the current of classroom living, sometimes steering, other times adrift. As part of a larger social and cultural web of meaning, we assume responsibility for many aspects of the process of identity formation; constructing as we are in turn constructed. But the world never stops long enough to provide any more than a fleeting glance of our selves. Moving. Somewhere else. We live with an ongoing, chronic sense of loss and hope, with the potential dis-ease of never-really-knowing. Who we are. But needing to know. Living under the old adage: *to steer is heaven, to drift is hell.*

It seems we must learn to be in two places at one time. Simultaneously. We must be in the river and also on the bank. This is *the curious time of pedagogy*. Of course, this is not necessarily news to the countless (self) reflective/reflexive souls, born out of several decades of productive dilemmas and mindful engagements with teaching and learning, who are constantly re-minding themselves and those they live and work with of the need to honor the complexity and the difficulty and the ambiguity of "making pathways through [the] world" (Greene 1995, 16). What *does* seem news-worthy, at least to me and to those I share classrooms with, is the possibilities that wordmaking and wordplay offer for making such pathways. For becoming a teacher. For becoming a learner. Infinite moments lived with delicacy and deliberateness. Moments. Waiting to be born. Waiting to be crushed. Crushed beneath the pedagogical weight that staggers even the imagination. And born out of that same weight that also gives wings and the possibility of weightlessness to those who might imagine otherwise.

My experience of writing and word-shopping with preservice teachers reminds me of the river and the river bank and gives me reason to think that we *can* be in both places at one time. Writing can create a "textual place for transformation" (Sumara and Davis 1997, 5), a place to consider this forever-stumbling as a necessary movement. Always on the way to somewhere else. Returning to Sumara's notion of the interpretive location, the writing-styled workshop (or word-shop) in teacher education offers opportunities to collect our experiences of living and teaching and learning and writing, opportunities to collect our selves. Paradoxically, the interpretive location points to how it is impossible to locate any of these acts in and of themselves. Rather, the invitation is to re/consider these acts in all their relations.

Britzman and Pitt's words continue to burn shadows—through this curious time of identity negotiation—into my writing (of) pedagogy...

> ... this may seem reminiscent of reflective practice...**casting the time of learning backward and forward**...something other than a linear recall...**a notion of time not yet recognized in teacher education**...how knowledge is constructed in moments of unresolve...**how to stage a pedagogy that is exploratory rather than content driven**...in cases of both assumed familiarity and unfamiliarity, what seems to be at stake is the teacher's sense of self. (Britzman and Pitt 1996, 117–123)

Some Notes to My Selves: "TeachingThroughWriting"

Journal Entry: The recasting of time in teacher education...the curious time of pedagogy: May 25, 1994. Another class finishes. Teacher candidates scribble quick notes called "exit slips" on scraps of paper which provide asked-for feedback to the instructor about how the course is going for them. They drop them on the desk, and then they are gone.

July 16, 1997: Still writing. Still thinking about May 25, 1994. Rereading. "Exit slips." Quick notes. Scraps of paper. Sorting through teachers' writing lives. And now *I'm* writing teachers lives. Here's one, for example. The teacher candidate says, *"Part of*

me is scared to take a risk, yet the rest of me is saying—what could
possibly go wrong?" Striking. Is she talking about writing or about
teaching? "What could possibly go wrong?" In what ways will
my response to her question write this teacher's life? This is what
I am scribbling down
in my journal as the train skates across summer
leaves scrolling green
pages of grass and birch windandpines fields glass blue windows.

The journal waits,
not burning so much
as sitting there
like a cheque book or a
toothache.   Or a life waiting

to happen. A mirror
with a marred surface. Out the window
we see our selves reflected,

identity   fleeting, like poems
sliced into postcard
scenes that change more quickly
than we can write them
down...

Through Writing: Through-Writing: *ThroughWriting*

Let's forget our Selves as teachers
through writing
(poetry).

Let's remember our Selves as teachers
through writing
(poetry).

Discovering that remembering
and forgetting are how we
re-member our Selves.

Through writing: through-writing—
throughwriting as an ambulatory
pedagogical experience.

Through-writing as an ongoing
process of identity
negotiation—

on the way *through* to someplace
else   satisfyingly confusing   to be
on the way.

Poetry and pedagogy: more than just a play
of words   more than just
Wordplay:

making poetry—*making* pedagogy.
Identity negotiation—
writing *as-if* we were poets: pretend poets,

writing *as-if* we were teachers: pretend teachers.
We are always *laying a path while walking*, while writing, while
teaching,

walking the lines of our writing,
watching our words become
our Selves

forgetting and re-membering.
Reconceptualizing the hyphen
-ated space: student-teacher...

reworking   rewording
re: wording   reimagining student
teacher:

studentteacher...stuteachdenter...stedachenturte
making (up) words, making non-
sense in order to make

sense of our
selves, in order to see
our selves   differently.

July 17, 1997. More writing in my journal...

As I continue to reflect on our time spent together in the course, I'm continuing to entertain the possibility that maybe we "learned nothing." And I'm not stretching for cleverness here, nor for some nihilistic view of how we spend our time in teacher education. Instead I'm wondering out loud over the possible importance of forgetting as a way of re-membering or reconfiguring ourselves and our pedagogy. Is it conceivable that we need places of "time out," places of forgetting in teacher education in order to re-member ourselves? Might forgetting be a part of the dynamic of identity formation and negotiation in teacher education? Forgetting who we were/are/were in order to remember ourselves, differently. Perhaps playfulness is a serious part of this dynamic. Taking our selves less seriously, even if only for relatively short periods of time within the longer course—a lifetime—of becoming a teacher. Can play be/come an important form of work?

The research of Vivian Gussin Paley (1979, 1990), well-known author and early childhood educator, would answer this question in the affirmative. She points to the important role of play in the work of learning and teaching. Paley calls play "the original open-ended and integrated curriculum" (1979, 142) a "practicing of problems" which gives all members of the classroom "a sense of communal purpose" (1990, 80).

Throughout the course, I was always aware of the sense of play that took place each and every morning (despite the 8:00 A.M. start). The invitation, always, was to write and reflect, interrogate and celebrate the ways we write and are written. The generous allotment of time to engage in writing exercises outside of the classroom space, to "wander for wonder," or "look for language," two exercises that involved looking for poetry in the world, often seemed too good to be true. In fact, I became uneasy on occasion, thinking that maybe time was being given out too generously...

Journal entry within a journal entry:
May 18, 1994—second day of class...
Carl outlines the next writing exercise called "Wander for Wonder"... "feel free to leave the room," he says—"go wander outside (it *is* May in Vancouver after all), look for something wonderful. Sit for 15 minutes and write"...
(Note: As a general rule coffee breaks were tacked on to these outdoor writing activities, combined in a sense, so that edges between writing and coffee, coffee and writing would be given the opportunity to blur. Longer coffee? Longer writing? Somewhere in between?)
Afterward I wrote: Carl is being extremely generous with TIME. Overly generous? I'm wondering if the teacher candidates think he is a pushover. Maybe they'll take advantage of his generosity, take advantage of the course structure, go for one long coffee, linger with lattés instead of words. Perhaps they did on occasion, but I know that over the length of the course, teacher candidates writing (lives) came to life. They used this time, opened up to it, expanded into the time.
An e-mail exchange took place among a group of us in class around this issue of time and play and enjoyment and fun in class. (There were eight or nine other sections, in this very large running of the course, which apparently were not having near as much fun as our section seemed to be having.) One teacher candidate wrote:

> ... those outside of our experience view [our class] with suspicion. I was describing to someone this morning about what a great class we have and the response was, "Oh, you're in 'Playdough Leggo's' section. I heard it was slack-assed." It's a sad comment that people refer to a class in which I learned so much as being slack-assed just because it was fun. It fits with the concept that unless it is unpleasant, it's not for real...

Yes, despite those who consider work and play as distinct curricular entities, I believe we need to create a location that enables us to play with pedagogy, not just with words. A chance to play with the real: a time out, a breathing, a loosening, a reminder through play—through writing—that all of this

becoming a teacher is difficult work. And worthwhile work, too.
So go. Give yourself permission to stare at the shadowplay on the
side of the building for fifteen minutes, forty minutes, an hour.
Not instead of learning but because of learning. Give yourself to
the page. Move your pen across its whiteness where no words
have been written, where every word has been written. Write
your words to whatever rhythms the pen appears to hear. You
may end up with a quiet poem about a tiny window
of a world that opened because
you were there. Or, perhaps

other voices intrude—your own
loud (inner) voices with thoughts—
about an upcoming teaching practicum,
an idea for an assignment
the rent that's due,
lunch.

And so these pressing
exigencies become your
poem...

If writing is a composing—"composing a life"—as Mary
Catherine Bateson (1989) has so beautifully described it, then
maybe we need a place, a location, to compose ourselves.

It's difficult to remain composed in composition. If we are
going to compose ourselves, do we need to first learn to read and
write? Notes? Words? I believe we can become composers on the
way toward composition. We can make music before we know the
names of the notes, before we are familiar with lines and spaces.
We can learn to break the "rules of writing" before we necessarily
know what all the rules are.

If we learn to forget about the notes, learn to become less self-
conscious about the lines, we can be surprised, startled even, at
the sounds that "appear" as music. We begin to change our
"definition" of music, of poetry, of teaching. Our identity slides,
shifts...

Living Un/grammatically: A Poet's Pedagogical Soliloquy

In my work with preservice teachers I face daily a dilemma. My student-teachers come to me with an urgent practical agenda: What do I need to know in order to survive the world of school? In effect they want me to tell them how to fit into a world that they assume is structured like a grammar, with traditions and conventions and rules and patterns. They are seeking ways to conform to the pedagogic world as it has been written, but I hope they will seek ways to transform the pedagogic world, always written and always in the process of being written. I hope my student-teachers will seek ways to write, actively and deliberately and imaginatively, the pedagogic world of students and teachers. Of course, I acknowledge the sense of urgent need expressed by my student-teachers for practical strategies and advice that will sustain them in Monday morning's grade eight language arts class. My student-teachers live in the space of the hyphen which connects their identities as students and as teachers, not sure who they are, their sense of authority unsettled, rendered tentative and unsure, by hyphenated hybridization. But instead of fearing this place of the hyphen, I encourage my student-teachers to dance in the space of the hyphen, to explore the possibilities for new identities. I want them to learn to challenge the ways in which the world has been written for them, to know that they are not only written, but that they also write the world. I invite my students to write the unwritten sentences, the sentences that interrogate and subvert syntax and semantics, the sentences that create spaces where my students can live un/grammatically. (Leggo 1998, 172)

I chose to feature this particular passage because of the way I believe it underscores some of the dramatic tensions of working with teacher candidates. It points to the ways that teacher education can sometimes be/come driven by dichotomies unwittingly perpetrated by those who spend time together in the hyphenated spaces of learning-to-teach. After all, as those who work with student-teachers, we are *all* in the relational space of the hyphen. As teacher educators it is, relationally speaking, impossible to simply work with a group of people who are, themselves, in the unsteady space of hyphenation without being in that space ourselves. All of us live in and out of this space and, in turn, often live the space-as-dilemma in a complex and *serpentine* tangle. Perhaps, as Leggo suggests, learning to teach—the process of negotiating an elusive identity called "teacher"—might also involve learning to live *un/grammatically...*

Writing Un/grammatically—Living Un/grammatically: A Series of Identity Negotiations

The prefix *un* is generally used to mean *not* or *the opposite of* (e.g., unhappy), but the prefix *un* can also be used to add an intensive force, as in *unloosen*. This is the way that I use the prefix in un/grammatically—to add the intensive force that suggests that to live un/grammatically is to live ultimately with more attention to the spirit of grammar rooted in gramarye.[2] To be un/grammatical is to be *not* in accordance with the rules of grammar, not staying in place, but questioning the assigned place, disrupting the order of place. Yet to be ungrammatical also means asking where do these rules and principles come from, and what are they, and who knows them? To be in accord with the rules or principles of grammar is to acknowledge the ways that the rules are generated and created and transformed. And because the rules of grammar are written, they are always available for re/writing, always open to un/grammatical re/generation. Hence to be un/grammatical is ultimately to be grammatical, and being too strictly grammatical can only lead to the betrayal of the spirit of grammar/gramarye. (Leggo 1998, 175–176)

And because the rules of grammar are written, they are always available for re/writing. Work-shopping, then, offers a location in which to practice word-shopping, to practice writing and living with words; rethinking, reconceptualizing writing as a practice of rewriting—through wordplay—the practice of grammar—the grammar of writing and the grammar of living. This ongoing textual negotiation, the grammar of identity negotiation, becomes easily entangled in the lines of our living, that is, in the tangle of our lines and lives.

Trinh T. Minh-ha writes about the notion of a "sentence-thinker who radically questions the world through the

---

[2] A more in-depth exploration of the notion of "gramarye," introduced by Leggo within the ENED 426 experience, can be found in Leggo (1998, 169–184). Briefly, Leggo uses gramarye as an etymological root to grammar, related to the old French *gramaire* or learning. Leggo states, "Gramarye means magic, occult knowledge, alchemy, necromancy, and enchantment. Now I want to use this new (or old) notion of grammar to support a poetic return to language that subverts and disrupts and erects and deconstructs, always playful, always purposeful...I want to pursue gramarye which invites mystery and openness and poetry"...(1998, 174).

questioning of a how-to-write" (1989, 17). This seems a more radical notion of writing-to-learn than the one emphasized in the Language Across the Curriculum movement; it is a much more embodied form of writing to learn. Similarly, learning to live un/grammatically, in the context of teacher education, involves "sentence-thinkers" who radically question the world (of teaching) through the questioning of a how-to-write, *and* of a how-to-teach. Through writing. Minh-ha continues, "a sentence-thinker, yes, but one who so very often does not know how a sentence will end...And as there is no need to rush, just leave it open, so that it may later on find, or not find, its closure" (1989, 19). Minh-ha's jeweled cluster of words speaks worlds within the world of teacher education. Of *writing* teacher education. Of writing ourselves as teachers. In our negotiation of identity—in our writing of identity, *we so very often do not know how a sentence will end...and as there is no rush*
just leave it   open
so that it may later on find or   not find its
closure...

Living and writing un/grammatically brings our lines and lives together. And apart. This is potentially disturbing: we do not know how a sentence—or a life—will proceed, or end. Even so, we need to know; in this need we most often feel the "rush-to-apply" ourselves as teachers. As those who know. Our identification with teaching—our identity as "teacher"—is partially wrapped up in what we know (to be a teacher). This kind of teacher is, generally, one who knows, and we are, of course, always being written. The identity of "teacher" insistently overwrites our writing as though we are palimpsests only. (*It shows us the patterns we are weaving...*)

If we work-shop identity, experiment with lines and lives by a questioning of how-to-write and how-to-teach, we become sentence-thinkers who question the grammar of how we write and how we are written. Writing un/grammatically, we re-member our selves and our writing as "question marks"—as an ongoing questioning of marks—of markings that scratch the page written...

Writing Identity: Questioning the (Question) Mark(s)?

Aren't our identities always question-able?
Aren't our identities always marked
by questions? By a   question-
ing of the grammar of writing   identity?
How often we don't question
grammar. How often we simply identify
grammar as the rules—the lines we must follow in order to write
our lives—our living. For example:
When is a question mark a question
of identity? And when, if ever, is it simply a question
mark? that tells us what to do at the end of a sentence?
When we come to a "period," for example,
must we come to a full.   Stop?

The grammar of the line is also the grammar of the
life. The grammar of identity negotiation is (question) marked
with/by textual innuendo.

A question mark is also a symbol: ?
that enables us to question the marks
we scratch out as symbols and signs that signify
our living and our writing.

We can question these marks through living un
grammatically which is a writing-as-questioning,
a writing as-if we are always just learning to question
the line,   as-if we are always just learning to question
the living, so that we are always negotiating the lines of our living,
the living of our lines
as-if we are always just learning
to write   as-if   we are always
just learning to teach   as-if
we are always just learning…

Living and writing un/grammatically highlights
the performative nature of living,   of writing
the tangle of

identity negotiated by our lines and lives
through writing
throughwriting identity...

In addition, the grammar of psychoanalytic insight, through the work of Felman (1987), would suggest that we are always "mobilizing" many more signs than we know so that writing practice that includes word-shopping involves writing practice without necessarily knowing (all of) what we are doing.

As a form of writing practice, wildmind writing is itself un/grammatical. It is a kind of writing practice that explicitly invites writers to break the rules of writing; it is interesting to note, however, that the "breaking of rules" through writing practice, as Goldberg writes writing practice, can also lead to a convention or grammar of its own—an ungrammar that we begin to identify *differently* with on the page. An ungrammar that, with (writing) practice, begins to identify us differently on the page—enables us to begin to identify ourselves *differently* on the page. Goldberg's "rules" for writing practice are, themselves, rules for learning to live un/grammatically; they are, in a sense, un/rules:

keep your hand moving... lose control... be specific...don't think...don't worry about punctuation, spelling, grammar...you are free to write the worst junk...go for the jugular...

As Goldberg herself states, "writing practice will help you contact your first thoughts. Just practice and forget everything else" (1990, 4). So writing practice, as espoused by Goldberg, seems to involve a losing of yourself in order to find yourself—differently. In this way writing practice is itself an ongoing process of identity negotiation; it is both a living practice and a practice of/for living. This making and breaking of rules, this losing and finding, this forever moving, but with specificity, with detail—in the face of the particular—all play in the liminal space of the workshop, which itself houses "ongoing, shifting, ambiguous nests or communities of interrelations which are constantly in need of renewal, regeneration, rethinking" (Jardine 1994a, 510). Interesting, too, how so many teacher candidates find it so terribly difficult *not* to follow the rules of learning to write and, significantly—of learning to write the life of teaching—even with the most generous of invitations. A workshop, in the context of teacher education, helps to collect our experience of learning to live a life that includes writing and teaching and learning—to write, to teach, to learn. The ways that we play with words create new conditions of learning that show us some of the ways we come to understand ourselves.

Trying on rules. Trying on roles.

Invited to write poetry, we tighten up. When we call it wordplay, however—simply another form of (writing) practice, a form of practice in which we begin to practice calling our writing poetry—we tend to loosen. The invitation into poetry, as our class came to understand and interpret poetry, as a group engaged in wordplay proved to be wonderfully writerly in its invitation to question the lie of the line, sometimes by questioning linearity, by breaking up the line, disrupting the lines with our lives. Disrupting our lives with our lines. Wordplay offered a generous textual form; it left openings for interpretation, it encouraged experimentation.

It's a fine line: we are our words, we are not our words. The only certainty seems to be the uncertain lines drawn between "categories" we have come to call private and public, playful and serious. "Following the line" has sometimes taken preservice teachers to places they may not have expected. To lived experiences remembered both painfully *and* playfully. Writing—one word after the other—has also led to a reconfiguring of certain lived experiences in ways that enable us to view ourselves differently. Private and playful. Intimate and public. Or, none of these. A writing exercise can trigger a string of words that we might then choose to work with—as earnest autobiography, as lavish fiction, as poetry, as essay, as story, as lavish autobiography, as earnest fiction. Moving forward and backward with words toward a place there are sometimes no words for. Writing the cliff

in order to climb up or step   off...

"Word-shopping": *Writing* Identity

This is the classroom on edge, everyone afraid of falling off. (Doll 1997, 72)

Everyone afraid of falling off. Or happy to explore the fall, to explore falling. Writing practice (including wildmind writing) in a writing workshop-styled setting—a place-turned-space where preservice teachers wrote together and shared their words with one another—sometimes felt like falling. The experience, though, of engaging in writing exercises together through intense periods of time, within any given session as well as over the extended time of the course, also offered opportunities to think about falling in directions other-than-down. The experience of writing alone and in small groups, of shaping freewriting into poetry and other genres, of interrogating language use within various subject disciplines, of reading words aloud to one another—all of these curricular acts were a way of becoming curious about learning, about writing, about teaching, about falling. The experience of writing practice created conditions of learning that further enabled us to become curious about our own experience of the practice of writing—of writing practice.

Certainly, a very common occurrence for many of us in the workshop was to experience writing as a kind of stumbling. Writing-as-stumbling: there was a sense in which this kind of writing was accidental in nature—a stumbling on to something. Sometimes this "something" was experienced as "nothing" in particular. Stan Dragland, citing Don McKay in his introduction to *Poetry and Knowing* (1995) states, "Poetry makes nothing happen. Nothing that happens is something, something we have never been able to recognize" (10). And so our words offered ways of working with "nothing." Nothing being, perhaps, those things we are unaware of until writing practice brings them forward into our practice of writing. Of reading our own writing differently. Making ourselves aware. Becoming aware of ourselves. Ourselves, *making* awareness.

The metaphorical image of "stumbling" made more visible in/through writing process offers a way to think about learning, and learning to negotiate identity, in which stumbling is a requisite part of the process. Stumbling is serendipitous.

Stumbling is movement—sometimes sudden—in which we aren't necessarily walking or falling, neither and both. We are neither upright nor fallen. Neither vertical nor horizontal. Neither here nor there. Stumbling calls for immediate adjustments and leads to places we can't always anticipate. The result can sometimes lead to a "happy accident," other times to an unanticipated fall. Writing practice invites us to suspend judgment on the fall; it creates conditions that enable us to consider this in-between place for writing and learning and teaching. Within the context of teacher education, writing within the workshop space enabled many of us to become less self-conscious about falling and in turn to become more conscious of the selves that are caught up in an ambulatory kind of identity negotiation and formation: writing "as-if" we were teachers. A sometimes stumbling. Toward teaching. Learning always.

"Following the line," then, is serious
wordplay that can lead to a
con-fuse-ion, a tangling
of lines and   lives.

Writing practice *itself* can create
a commonplace location—a chunk of words that enables us
to see our selves fashioned
through form. When we write
with wildmind we often see our own writing
differently
as the lines fall out in ways
that catch our   ear, attract the   eye
allow us to think about calling our writing
poetry.

This "poetry," then, can become a kind of poetry of practice, a poetics of practice, if you will. When we practice writing we gain insight into our writing and our learning and our teaching as it becomes visible to us. We become curious about our writing and our learning and our teaching. Our writing helps us to locate ourselves between knowing and not knowing. Closer to knowing what we don't know we know which brings us closer

to knowing.　　　Re-membering that knowing is "a weave of knowing
and not-knowing" (Spivak, in Lather, revisited).

Word-shopping becomes writing as if
teacher education was an imagining. Writing
as-if we were teachers. Writing as-if we were
poets caught up in a poem
unending in which learning is
everything
and we can't imagine
it　　　otherwise. Word-shopping becomes (more than) just
wordplay; it becomes...

Learning to teach through writing...**Learning** to write through writing...**Learning** to **learn** through writing...**Learning** to teach through **learning**...**Learning** to write through **learning**...**Learning** to **learn** through **learning**...**Learning** to teach through teaching...**Learning** to write through teaching...**Learning** to **learn** through teaching...Writing to **learn** through writing...Writing to teach through writing...Writing to write through writing...Writing to **learn** through learning...Writing to teach through **learning**...Writing to write through **learning**...Writing to **learn** through teaching...Writing to teach through teaching...Writing to write through teaching...Teaching to **learn** through **learning**...Teaching to write through **learning**...Teaching to teach through **learning**...Teaching to **learn** through writing...Teaching to write through writing...Teaching to teach through writing...Teaching to **learn** through teaching...Teaching to write through teaching...Teaching to teach through teaching...

Word-shopping is thinking
about Jeanette Winterson's
words:　　　*The rope is*
hand produced
the writer makes it
as she walks　　*it* (1996, 161).

Word-shopping is Imagining
we could perform
a never-ending   interchange of
w r i t e r   w i t h   ⚲ t e a c h e r   w i t h
learner...withwriterwithteacherwithlearnerwithteacherwithwriter
withlearnerwithlearnerwithwriterwithteacherwithlearnerwithteac
herwithwriterwithlearnerwithlearnerwithwriterwithteacherwithle
arnerwithteacherwithwriterwithlearnerwithlearnerwithwriterwith
teacherwithlearnerwithteacherwithwriterwithlearnerwithlearner
withwriterwithteacherwithlearnerwith
teacherwithwriter
withlearnerwithlearner
withteacher
with...
Word-shopping is Imagining a life
that includes
writing.

* * *

   Madeleine Grumet argues that "the personal is a performance,
an appearance [or mask] contrived for the public" (1995, 37). She
further argues that "these masks enable us to perform the play of
pedagogy" (37). Similarly, word-shopping offered an invitation to
write in ways that enabled teacher candidates to "perform"
pedagogy through an act of doing, an act of making. Masks. Of
making insight. Making words. Wordmaking. Making identity.
Masking identity. The workshop promoted what science educator
David Hawkins has called a kind of "messing about"...a "free and
unguided exploratory work (call it play if you wish, [says
Hawkins] I call it work)" with language (Hawkins 1974, 38).
Preservice teachers were thus able to try different (teaching) selves
on for size through wordplay.
   Grumet's essay is part of an important collection of essays
which attempt to re-think pedagogy "at the place where the
personal becomes impersonation" (Gallop 1995, 2). The work of
Gallop and her colleagues, when read alongside the ENED 426
workshop experience, helps to break down some of the traditional
binaries of personal (where personal equals authentic) and

impersonation (where impersonation equals a false performance). The result of this collapse is a new, hyphenated term, "im-personation": "a new configuration in which the personal and the mask are not mutually exclusive alternatives" (Gallop 1995, 8). This is tricky ground. My intention is not to mask the fear of becoming a teacher but, rather, to give this fear a different face. The workshop is, after all, about lines and lives, real lives to whom we are responsible in our roles as teachers and researchers and meaningmakers. This is not about teacher education pretend. Gallop (1995) provides some reassurance, however, in her reminder that "[t]he scare quotes around 'pretends'...suggest that the student is not simply pretending, that the student is in some way 'really' in the position [s]he is impersonating" (6).

Following Gallop, the workshop was thus a location in which to "raise the spectre of a less-than-certain self exposed by a fascinating array of poststructural fashions" (Willinsky 1990, 221), in which language is used not so much to reveal as it is to create a self. The self in this instance, is constructed, negotiated, shared. This can be an unsettling experience, particularly if we are looking for a self "that reeks of 'authenticity,' 'sincerity,' and discloses privileged glimpses into the human heart" (Graham 1991, 149). Within the workshop walls, however, this slippery sense of self also proved to be liberating with its "potential to ease the responsibility and the burden of autobiography as a solemn process of psychotherapy, or a self-righteous thrust towards empowerment" (Rasberry 1993, 8). The intent of much of the personal writing of the preservice teachers—the literacy narratives, the poetry, the storying—was therefore not always aimed at a "deadly coherence" (Grumet 1995, 38). (Though a good deal of the writing was, in fact, raw, emotionally charged material.) There was a sense in which the writing allowed teacher candidates to "act out"—or in a less Freudian sense of wordplay—to act on their ideas for teaching, to participate in an ongoing pedagogical play, to go word-shopping—for a self, for a living, for a life that included teaching. Preservice teachers were, in this way, able to write their way in and out of the largely inherited and often constraining context of the teacher education program. They were encouraged to experiment with the multiple roles and identities of teacher: critiquing, celebrating, problematizing. In a very direct and immediate fashion, language offered a way for preservice teachers to find some of their own ways across the curriculum.

Wordplay offers a text—readerly, writerly, and researcherly—that helps create "curricular locations for the interpretation of the teaching identities student teachers negotiate as they learn to teach" (Sumara and Luce-Kapler 1996, 65). And further, keeping with Sumara and Luce-Kapler's work, wordplay, through writing practice, highlights "the need to become creative with the print texts used in teacher education"(Sumara and Luce-Kapler 1996, 71). Writing practice, framed within the growing body of research in teacher education that continues to interpret identity negotiation, offers, in the words of Jill McClay (1997) at the University of Alberta, "expanded and expansive conceptions of the roles of writing in our learning." As McClay notes, these kinds of writing practices "offer beginning teachers both forum and form for the creation of new fictions, new narratives for their teaching lives" (McClay 1997, 10). McClay's work, stated most clearly in the title of her essay, "Writing Lines to Compose Ourselves: Performing Fictionalized Identities," offers parallels to the work-shop experience of teacher candidates where "writing itself also serves as a locus offering space and possibility in which to develop identities as writers and teachers...their writings become sites for re-consideration of their experiences of learning and teaching" (McClay 1997, 1).

Wordplay can help teacher candidates perform the difficult work of identity negotiation. The practice of writing—to learn or to teach or research—is a practice of creating conditions that enable one to continue to practice writing—to teach or to learn or to research. Learning and teaching and researching, then, become a life practice. In turn, a reading that offers an invitation to experience a life that includes the practice of writing and researching, teaching and learning, is not an invitation to experience the completion of any of these inextricable parts of our living; it is, rather, an invitation to a tangled journey into the curious time of pedagogy that is never complete, will never be complete.

Fanzined Closure:
A Complex Gathering of Citations, Incantations, and Ruminations in Endless Combinations and Permutations

At the edges, where lines are blurred, it is easier to imagine that the world might be different. (Bateson 1989, 73)

Painting is trying to paint. What you cannot paint. And writing is what you cannot know. Before you have written. It is preknowing. And not knowing. Blindly. With words...**We can take a class from a writer, but it is not enough. We can't make that kamikaze leap. So writing is always over there...**We can rest and float. Move and yet not move...**Imagine**...Through the tangle. Teachers' writing lives. **Through the tangle.** Teachers *writing* lives. **A curricular location for teacher candidates to imagine education through a life that includes writing.** To imagine education through poets' I's: **I want to be like the girl with the flashlight.** Through educators' eyes. **To imagine:** *Here is a broad stone wall flicking alive small green flames of lizards. The wall is low. We sit on its back watching the road that curves around the wet blue belly of the sea.* **Imagine**...This is what I find when I look back. Over my shoulder. Toward the future. **A record of obsession.** A bowl of yellow flowers. *The sea is always itself. Restless. Forever altering. Its colours. Like a sad eye. The road itself. Never shifts. The squat wall I balance on...***Wait here.** For. Some kind of unfolding. **Word upon word.** I cannot yet say what this something is. **Maybe it's only the promise.** The tangle. **Immersed.** Entangled. **Complicit.** Can a study of the self? **S t u d y i n g education.** Create. **New conditions.** Of learning. And the making. **Of pedagogical insight?** Imagine instead a blank space on the wall—**a perfectly empty circle** that does not return our watch-full stares. I want my students to see **the universe of language.** Recognizable, like stars floating liquid on a dark surface. **Painting is trying to paint.** What you cannot paint. **And writing.** Is what you cannot know. Before you have written. **A weave of knowing.** And not-knowing. Which is what knowing is. The tangle is itself. **Blindly with words.** A **fanzine.** Simply. A complex gathering.

Through writing. *Through*writing. A mirror. Writing reflects. **Tangled Lines and Lives.** Becoming **curious.** Through a poet's I. A life. Lives. Ambiguity. Every statement we make in educational writing. Must be able to be read. As the answer. To a question. **That could have been answered otherwise.** Self-reflexivity. **Never.** Does one open. The discussion. **By coming right to the heart.** Of the matter. The heart of the matter. Is always somewhere else. **To write. As if your life. Depended on it.** No real beginning. Middle. End. **Curriculum** *Objects*. This study is part of my doctoral research. You may refuse to participate. Please indicate your consent. At least not a 20 out of 20 poet. **Yes, you are sure now about the wall.** The wall is why you have come. Putting the hex on cliché. Whisper the incantation as it was given. **Words fall.** Plant themselves. **Waiting for the world.** To imagine itself. **Out of a seed.** Or run. Its course. **Like an avalanche.** Down a garden **path**. Ripping up **color**. As it goes…

the reflexive practitioner
(a self-reflexive aside)

a next to last
INTERLUDE

The Reflexive Practitioner: A Self-Reflexive Aside

Is it NOT reelee onlee a bunch of words...[?] (bisset 1993, 40)

WaRniNg: Wordplay is Full of Adumbrations that May Cause Excessive Wordplay...

Turning curiosity
into (a turning that is) a

tangle is (not) always (or

necessarily)
                                        recommended
and may cause excessive
tangling that can often lead
to the need for serious
textual un/tangling

which is by way of saying that

a tangle of lines and lives can often lead to the
curious   practice   of
    Footnoting...³

---

³ "Freudian slips"— A Play-Full Footnote for 2 Voices:
voice1: Is it just me   or have I used a(n) (awful) lot of brackets in the (word)making of this book? voice2: *No, you have. Definitely. voice1*: What does this mean do you think?   voice2: *I think it means whatever you'd like it to mean. voice1*: No, seriously. Not "the-readerly/writerly text" again, please. voice2: *OK then, it's likely because (being) (in) the tangle means (that) meaning gets really tangled. There are so many possible meanings that it gets quite difficult—(tangled, if you will)—to decide which meaning you mean...the "signify-ability syndrome" becomes a factor.* Yes, you're right, that's it. *Yes, so you (begin to) introduce (some) brackets to help ensure that the poetic neurons are firing at appropriate speeds through multiple (tangled) pathways.* Yes, I see what you mean. Anyway, I see now that as I move deep/er into the tangle, the pathways seem more complex, right? (Write?) *Right. And (more) ambiguous, too.* And, questionable, even? *Yes, in a strange sense; there will be*

---

a lot more questions possible and a lot more possible questions. Lots of strange opt/ions: (a) weird way(s) to indicate meaning(s). Some readers won't like it one bit. They'll ask, Why so many brackets? It makes it hard(er) to read! It makes (for) (a) (crazy) read(er)ing: rendering. But others will get into it. Open (up) to it. Think (it's) open. Readerly. Roll with/in—(with) (in)—waves. Writerly. Following the line, just like it was a line from a set of cryptic line(r) (notes). Others will [(think) (it's)] refuse to read (it). They'll claim it makes no(n)sense. They'll say that it's closed. They'll say it's hermetic not hermeneutic. Herme(n)(eu)tic. Some will think it's just plain questionable to write words this small in a footnote and expect others to read it.

the refractive practitioner
(a scientific poem of refrangibility)

_____ a last
INTERLUDE

The Refractive Practitioner:
A Scientific Poem of Refrangibility

1. ReFrAnGiBLe: *capable of being refracted.*   Capable   of
bending, of
                                                  changing
direction in passing obliquely from one medium into
    another…
                        The poet's I which is (also)
                        the poet's eye—like any other eye
                        is able to refract light so that upon entering
the eye
    light forms   an image that appears on the retina.
According to the
                        refrangible theory of wordplay, then,
                        the practice of writing, or writing practice
helps
    create new conditions which help the eye—and the "I'—to
learn
                                                    to
refract light in ways that enable it to form images on the retina:
differently. Further, this theory of   wordplay
    suggests that the poet's I is not a privileged I. The poet is not
necessarily one who sees   differently.   All eyes have
it. [Or, by way of wordplay (if we were to take a vote):
    the eyes have it.]   All eyes—all I's—are able
to practice writing.   Practice learning.   Practice
teaching.   Practice learning to bend light so as to see the
world in words. The I's, through writing, throughwriting, can
learn to create new conditions for further learning. To write. To
learn. To write to learn. To practice. And
    even   further: poetry is in the eye of the beholder.
The I of the beholder:
            Beautee is in the I of the bee-holder as we begin to buzz
with wordplay.

2. ReFrAcToRy: *Hard or impossible to manage:* like the tangle.
Resisting ordinary methods.

A theory of refrangibility suggests
  that the refrangible practitioner would be
well-suited to pass through   the tangle   yet the tangle
is itself a refrangible   object   so that each
time one practices theory it changes
unpredictably   due to the refrangibility
factor which in turn causes one's theory to practice differently
in each passing   through   the tangle.
As it turns out this is a curious way
to research writing. A curious
way for writing research:
through a poet's   I…

POSTSCRIPT

Closure is hard to imagine.

—John Moss, *Enduring dreams*, 1996.

Kingston writer Kent Nussey says,

the practice of writing, the extended act of creation, might cost the writer the very things he's trying to capture and illumine in his writing (1993).

What becomes pedagogical in this postscript, read backward and forward through the preface, is what the curious time of researching pedagogy has both offered and demanded of a study of a self studying education: the possibility of both losing and finding oneself within the curious pedagogical relations made possible through the self's encounter—both with its own otherness, as well as with the otherness of others (Britzman 1998). My own belief, as these words begin to point toward closure, is that the practice of writing costs, but never does it diminish the worth of experiencing the richness of the in-between place, the place between living and writing—the space that makes both possible.

I now live with/in the tangled conviction that any life that includes the practice of writing offers opportunities to read the above words from Kent Nussey *differently* each time. As if for the first time. The practice of writing—writing practice—is writing pedagogy that writes pedagogy with both promise and portent. It is not fear or desire that compel us to put one word after the other in order to compose our selves and our living, but fear *and* desire. Always the unsettling juxtaposition of opposites. Always the necessary risk of moving through the deeply ambivalent living that is somehow part of how we imagine our everydayness. Through the tangled experience of living a life that includes the practice of writing.

What *is* the experience of living a life that includes the practice of writing? The shortest route, through the tangle, to an answer might read *it depends*, an answer which might be read as a tangle of postmodern playfulness with hermeneutic

underpinnings, a poetic
rendering informed by psychoanalytic
insight, an existential quandary scratched
by the curious time
of researching pedagogy, a bowl of yellow
flowers through a poet's I.
A theoretical practice, a practicing of theory, a wildmind
writing exercise (aka, a five-year timed-writing), a seriously long
poem, a piece of researcherly fiction, a piece of fictional research,
an epistemological stumbling toward quiddity, a pedagogical
offering open to   interpretation.

All of these, perhaps, but in the end it is as David Jardine
suggests, an answer to a question that can always be answered
otherwise. Meantime, "I have taken my eye off the world to write
about it," cut myself off from pedagogy in order to write about it.
I have discovered the writing of this practice and the practice of
this writing to be a richly ambiguous experience, troubling at
times in its contradictions, but most times a satisfyingly obsessive
way to forever practice living. (While forever living practice.)

The curious time of researching pedagogy. Not just
researching writing. But writing research. Yes. Of course. This is
how it must begin:

words falling
on open fields, planting
themselves and waiting
for the world
to imagine
itself out of a seed or run
its course like
an avalanche
down a
garden
path
ripping up
color as it
goes...

REFERENCES

Aoki, T. (1997). Foreword. *Educational Insights*, 4(1)
http://www.csci.educ.ubc.ca/publication/insights/index.html

Atwood, M. (1995). *Morning in the burned house.* Toronto: McLelland & Stewart.

Bakhtin, M. (1981). *The dialogic imagination.* Austin: University of Texas.

Barthes, R. (1975). *The pleasure of the text.* New York: Hill & Wang.

Barthes, R. (1987). The plural text/the plural self, *College English* 49(2): 158–170.

Bateson, M.C. (1989). *Composing a life.* New York: Penguin.

Berlak, A.C. (1996). Teaching stories: Viewing a cultural diversity course through the lens of narrative. *Theory Into Practice* 35(2). 93–101.

Berry, W. (1983). *Standing by words.* San Francisco: North Point Press.

Bishop, W. and Ostrom, H. (Eds.) (1994). *Colours of a different horse: Rethinking creative writing theory and pedagogy.* Urbana, Illinois: National Council of Teachers of English.

bisset, b. (1993). *th last photo uv th human soul.* Vancouver: Talonbooks.

Bowering, G. and Hutcheon, L. (Eds.) (1992). *Likely stories: A postmodern sampler.* Toronto: Coach House Press.

Britzman, D. (1991). *Practice makes practice: A critical study of learning to teach.* Albany: SUNY Press.

Britzman, D. (1998). *Lost subjects, contested objects: Toward a psychoanalytic inquiry of learning.* Albany, NY: SUNY Press.

Britzman, D. and Pitt, A. (1996). Pedagogy and transference: Casting the past of learning into the presence of teaching, *Theory Into Practice* 35(2): 117–123.

Britzman, D., Dippo, D., Searle, D., and Pitt, A. (1995). *Report of the academic framework committee.* Toronto, ON: Faculty of Education, York University.

Calkins, L. M. (1991). *Living between the lines.* Portsmouth, NH: Heinemann.

Calvino, I. (1981). *If on a winter's night a traveller.* Toronto, ON: Lester & Orpen Dennys Ltd.

Caputo, J. (1987). *Radical hermeneutics: Repetition, deconstruction, and the hermeneutic project.* Bloomington, IN: Indiana University Press.

Castlebury, J. (Ed.) (1995). *Windhorse reader.* Yarmouth, NJ: Samurai Press.

Chambers, C. (1996). Composition and composure. Unpublished paper presented at WESTCAST, Saskatoon, SK.

Chambers, C. (1998). Composition and composure. *Alberta English* 36(2): 21–27.

Cixous, H. (1993). *Three steps on the ladder of writing.* New York: Columbia University Press.

Cohen, L. (1993). *Stranger music: Collected poems and songs.* Toronto, ON: McClelland & Stewart, Inc.

Coles, W. (1978). *The plural I.* New York: Holt.

Connelly, K. (1993). A bowl of yellow flowers stains the canvas. *This brighter prison: A book of journeys.* London, ON: Brick Books.

Connelly, K. (1995). *One room in a castle: Letters from Spain, France and Greece.* Winnipeg, MB: Turnstone Press.

Cook, M. (1995). Water, falling. In J. Castlebury (Ed.), *Windhorse reader.* Yarmouth, NJ: Samurai Press.

Crane, D. (1995). A personal postscript. In J. Gallop (Ed.), *Pedagogy: The question of impersonation* (pp. ix–xiv). Bloomington, IN: Indiana University Press.

Crowhurst, M. (1994). Language and learning across the curriculum. Scarborough, ON: Allyn & Bacon.

Davis, B. (1996). *Teaching mathematics: Toward a sound alternative.* New York: Garland.

Denzin, N. and Lincoln, Y. (Eds.) (1994). *Handbook of qualitative research.* Thousand Oaks, CA: Sage.

Dewey, J. (1934). *Art as experience.* New York: Perigee Books.

Dillard, A. (1989). *The writing life.* New York: HarperPerennial.

Dillard, A. (1982). *Living by fiction.* New York: HarperPerennial.

Doll, M. A. (1995). *To the lighthouse and back: Writings on teaching and living.* New York: Peter Lang.

Doll, M. A. (1997). Winging it. *Journal of Curriculum Theorizing* 13(1): 41–44.

Dragland, S. (1995). Introduction: Lunch and hunger. In T. Lilburn (Ed.), *Poetry and knowing: Speculative essays and interviews* (pp. 9–16). Kingston, ON: Quarry Press.

Elbow, P. (1981). *Writing with power: Techniques for mastering the writing process.* New York: Oxford University Press.

Ellsworth, E. (1996). Situated response-ability to student papers. *Theory Into Practice* 35(2): 138–143.

Felman, S. (1987). *Jacques Lacan and the adventure of insight. Psychoanalysis in contemporary culture.* Cambridge, MA: Harvard University Press.

Fine, M. (1994). Working the hyphens: Reinventing self and other in qualitative research. In N. Denzin and Y. Lincoln (Eds.), *Handbook of qualitative research* (pp. 70–82). Thousand Oaks, CA: Sage, 1994.

Florio-Ruane, S. and Lensmire, T. (1990). Transforming future teachers' ideas about writing instruction. *Journal of Curriculum Studies* 22 (3): 277–289.

Friedman, B. (1993). *Writing past dark: Envy, fear, distraction, and other dilemmas in the writer's life.* New York: HarperPerennial.

Gadamer, H. (1976). *Philosophical hermeneutics.* Los Angeles: University of California Press.

Gallop, J. (1995). Im-Personation: A reading in the guise of an introduction. In J. Gallop (Ed.), Pedagogy: The question of impersonation (pp. 1–18). Bloomington: Indiana University Press.

Gass, W. (1979). The world within the word. Boston: Nonpareil Books, 1979.

Glover, D. (1992). Dog attempts to drown man in Saskatoon. In G. Bowering and L. Hutcheon (Eds.), Likely stories: A postmodern sampler (pp. 111–131). Toronto: Coach House Press.

Goldberg, N. (1986). Writing down the bones: Freeing the writer within. Boston: Shambala Publications.

Goldberg, N. (1990). Wild mind: Living the writer's life. New York: Bantam Books.

Graham, R. J. (1991). Reading and writing the self: Autobiography in education and the curriculum. New York: Teachers College Press.

Graves, D. (1983). Writing: Teachers and children at work. Portsmouth, NH: Heinemann.

Greene, M. (1994). Postmodernism and the crisis of representation. English Education 26(4): 206–219.

Greene, M. (1995). Releasing the imagination: Essays on education, the arts and social change. San Francisco: Jossey-Bass.

Grigg, R. (1994). The Tao of Zen. Boston, MA: Charles E. Tuttle Press.

Grumet, M. (1995). Scholae personae: Masks for meaning. In J. Gallop (Ed.), Pedagogy: The question of impersonation (pp. 36–45). Bloomington: Indiana University Press.

Grumet, M. (1988). Bittermilk: Women and teaching. Amherst: University of Massachusetts Press.

Harris, J. (1987). The plural text/the plural self. College English 49(2): 158–170.

Hawkins, D. (1974). The informed vision: Essays on learning and human nature. New York: Agathon Press.

Hillman, J. (1979). Senex and puer: An aspect of the historical and psychological present. In J. Hillman (Ed.), *Puer papers* (pp. 3–53). Dallas: Spring Publications.

Hillman, J. (1989). *A blue fire. Selected writings*. New York: HarperPerennial.

Hillman, J. (1992). Speaking well and speaking out. In R. Bly, J. Hillman, and M. Meade (Eds.), *The rag and bone shop of the heart* (pp. 151–159). New York: HarperCollins.

Hillman, J. (1996). *The soul's code in search of character and calling*. New York: Random House.

hooks, b. (1994). *Teaching to transgress: Education as the practice of freedom*. New York: Routledge.

Hutcheon, L. (1992). Canada's 'post': Sampling today's fiction. In G. Bowering and L. Hutcheon (Eds.), *Likely stories: A postmodern sampler* (pp. 9–15). Toronto: Coach House Press.

Ignatieff, M. (1993). *Scar tissue*. Toronto: Penguin.

Jardine, D. (1992a). *Speaking with a boneless tongue*. Bragg Creek, AB: Makyo Press.

Jardine, D. (1992b). The fecundity of the individual case: considerations of the pedagogic heart of interpretive work. *Journal of Philosophy of Education*, 26(1): 51–61.

Jardine, D. (1992c). Reflections of education, hermeneutics, and ambiguity: Hermeneutics as a restoring of life to its original difficulty. In W. F. Pinar and W. M. Reynolds (Eds.), *Understanding curriculum as phenomenological and deconstructed text* (pp. 116–127). New York: Teachers College Press.

Jardine, D. (1993). Wild hearts, silent traces, and the journeys of lament. *The Journal of Educational Thought*, 27(1): 18–27.

Jardine, D. (1994a). 'Littered with literacy': An ecopedagogical reflection on whole language, pedocentrism and the necessity of refusal. *Journal of Curriculum Studies*, 26(5): 509–524.

Jardine, D. (1994b). Student-teaching, interpretation and the monstrous child. *Journal of Philosophy of Education*, 28(1): 17–24.

Jardine, D. (1995a). The stubborn particulars of grace. In B. Horwood (Ed.), *Experience and the curriculum* (pp. 261–275). Dubuque, Iowa: Kendall/Hunt Publishing Co.

Jardine, D. (1995b). The profession needs new blood: Interpretation, rites of renewal and the case of student-teaching. *Journal of Curriculum Theorizing*, 11 (3): 105–130.

Jardine, D. and Field, J. (1992). "Disproportion, monstrousness, and mystery": Ecological and ethical reflections on the initiation of student-teachers into the community of education. *Teaching and Teacher Education*, 8(3): 301–310.

Jerome, J. (1989). *Stone work: Reflections on serious play and other aspects of country life.* New York: Penguin Books.

Kundera, M. (1986). *The art of the novel.* New York: Harper & Row.

Lather, P. (1991). *Getting smart: Feminist research and pedagogy with/in the postmodern.* New York: Routledge.

Lather, P. and Ellsworth, E. (1996). This issue: Situated pedagogies—classroom practices in postmodern times. *Theory Into Practice*, 35(2): 70–71.

Lee, D. (1995). Writing in colonial space. In B. Ashcroft, G. Griffiths, and H. Tiffin (Eds.), *The Post-colonial studies reader* (pp. 397–401). London and New York: Routledge.

Leggo, C. (1992). A poet's pensées: Writing and schooling. *English Quarterly*, 23(3–4): 4–10.

Leggo, C. (1996). Dancing with desire: A meditation on psychoanalysis, politics and pedagogy. *Teachers and teaching: theory and practice*, 2(2): 233–242.

Leggo, C. (1998). Living un/grammatically in a grammatical world: The pedagogic world of teachers and students. *Interchange*, 29(2): 169–184.

Leggo, C. and Rasberry, G. W. (1995). Naming wounds-healing wounds: Working with wounded writers, *Textual Studies in Canada*, 7, 86–95.

Lensmire, T. (1994a). *When children write: Critical re-visions of the writing workshop.* New York: Teachers College Press.

Lensmire, T. (1994b). Writing workshop as carnival: Reflections on alternative learning environments. *Harvard Educational Review*, 64(4): 371–391.

Lensmire, T. (1995). Rewriting student voice. Paper presented at the American Educational Research Association Annual Meeting, San Francisco, CA.

Lightman, A. (1993). *Einstein's dreams*. New York: Warner Books.

Lilburn, T. (Ed.) (1995). *Poetry and knowing: Speculative essays and interviews*. Kingston, ON: Quarry Press.

Lineham, D. (1995). The earth makes announcements. In J. Castlebury (Ed.), *Windhorse reader*. Yarmouth, NJ: Samurai Press.

Livingston, M.C. (1990). *Climb into the bell tower: Essays on poetry*. New York: Harper & Row.

Lundy, J. (1994). WAC and institutional change. In C. Schryer and L. Steven (Eds.), *Contextual literacy: Writing across the curriculum* (pp. 64–76). Winnipeg, MB: Inkshed.

Maimon, E. (1994). Writing across the curriculum: History and future. In C. Schryer and L. Steven (Eds.), *Contextual literacy: Writing across the curriculum* (pp. 12–20). Winnipeg, MB: Inkshed Publications.

Marshall, B.K. (1992). *Teaching the postmodern: Fiction and theory*. New York: Routledge.

McClay, J. (1997). Writing lines to compose ourselves: Performing fictionalized identities. Unpublished paper presented at the American Educational Research Conference, Chicago, IL.

McKay, D. (1995). Baler twine: Thoughts on ravens, home, and nature poetry. In T. Lilburn (Ed.), *Poetry and knowing: Speculative essays and interviews* (pp. 17–28). Kingston, ON: Quarry Press.

Michaels, A. (1995). Cleopatra's love. In T. Lilburn (Ed.), *Poetry and knowing: Speculative essays and interviews* (pp. 177–183). Kingston, ON: Quarry Press.

Minh-ha, Trinh T. (1989). Woman, native, other. Bloomington, IN: Indiana University Press.

Morrison, P. and Morrison, P. (1982). Powers of ten. About the relative size of things in the universe. New York: Scientific American Library.

Moss, J. (1996). Enduring dreams: An exploration of Arctic landscape. Concord, ON: Anansi Press.

Murray, D. (1985). A writer teaches writing. Boston: Houghton Mifflin.

Murray, D. (1990). Shoptalk: learning to write with writers. Portsmouth, N.H.: Boynton/Cook.

Neilsen, L. (1998). Knowing her place. San Francisco: Caddo Gap.

Nussey, K. (1993). The writing life and Winesberg's 'Book of the Grotesque'. Unpublished address presented to the Kingston School of Writing, Kingston, ON.

Nussey, K. (1997). The war in heaven. Toronto, ON: Insomniac Press.

Orner, M. (1996). Teaching for the moment: Intervention projects as situated pedagogy. Theory into Practice, 35(2): 72–78.

Ostrom, H. (1994). Introduction: Of radishes and shadows, theory and pedagogy. In W. Bishop and H. Ostrom (Eds.), Colours of a different horse: Rethinking creative writing theory and pedagogy (pp. xi–xxiii). Urbana, IL: National Council of Teachers of English.

Pagano, J. (1990). Exiles and communities. Albany: SUNY Press.

Paley, V. G. (1979). White teacher. Cambridge, MA: Harvard University Press.

Paley, V. G. (1990). The boy who would be a helicopter: The uses of storytelling in the classroom. Cambridge, MA: Harvard University Press.

Patton, A. (1995). A persistently dimming flashlight. In T. Lilburn (Ed.), Poetry and knowing: Speculative essays and interviews (pp. 149–160). Kingston, ON: Quarry Press.

Pitt, A. (1996). Fantasizing women in the women's studies classroom: Toward a symptomatic reading of negation. *JCT: A Journal of Interdisciplinary Studies*, 12(4): 32–40.

Rasberry, G. W. (1993). Crafting a life. Craft as an element in autobiographical writing. *Educational Insights*, 1(2): 5–9.

Rasberry, G. W. (1994). Trust me I'm a doctor: Healing the wounded writer? *English Quarterly*, 26(2): 17–20.

Rasberry, G. W. (1997). Finding form. *Journal of Curriculum Theorizing*, 13(4): 46–49.

Rasberry, G. W. and Jardine, D. (1995). Curriculum and the poetics of educational research. Book prospectus.

Rich, A. (1993). *What is found there: Notebooks on poetry and politics*. New York: Norton.

Richardson, L. (1994). Writing. A method of inquiry. In N. Denzin and Y. Lincoln (Eds.), *Handbook of qualitative research* (pp. 516–529). Thousand Oaks, CA: Sage.

Robertson, J. (1997). Screenplay pedagogy and the interpretation of unexamined knowledge in pre-service primary teaching. *Taboo*, 1 (Spring): 25–60.

Rooney, E. (1989). *Seductive reasoning: Pluralism as the problematic of contemporary literary theory*. Ithaca, NY: Cornell University Press.

Salvio, P. (1996). Reading and the politics of identity. *JCT: A Journal of Interdisciplinary Studies*, 12(4): 2–5.

Sarbo, L. and Moxley, J. (1994). Creativity research and classroom practice. In W. Bishop and H. Ostrom (Eds.), *Colours of a different horse. Rethinking creative writing theory and pedagogy* (pp. 133–145). Urbana, IL: National Council of Teachers of English.

Schaafsma, D. (1996). Things we cannot say: "Writing for your life" and stories in English education. *Theory into Practice*, 35 (2): 110–116.

Simon, R. (1992). *Teaching against the grain: Texts for a pedagogy of possibility*. New York: Bergin & Garvey.

Smith, D. (1994). *Pedagon: Meditations on pedagogy and culture.* Bragg Creek, AB: Makyo Press.

Sumara, D. (1995). Response to reading as a focal practice. *English Quarterly*, 28(1): 18–26.

Sumara, D. (1996a). *Private readings in public: Schooling the literary imagination.* New York: Peter Lang.

Sumara, D. (1996b). Using commonplace books in curriculum studies. *Journal of Curriculum Theorizing*, 12(1): 45–48.

Sumara, D. and Davis, B. (1996). Editors' notes. *Journal of Curriculum Theorizing*, 12(1): 2–5.

Sumara, D. and Davis, B. (1997). Editors' notes. *Journal of Curriculum Theorizing*, 13(1): 2–5.

Sumara, D. and Luce-Kapler, R. (1996). (Un)becoming a teacher: Negotiating Identities while learning to teach. *Canadian Journal of Education*, 21(1): 65–83.

Wallace, B. (1987). *The stubborn particulars of grace.* Toronto: McClelland and Steward.

Watterson, B. (1988). *Scientific progress goes "boink."* Kansas City: Andrews and McMeel.

Willinsky, J. (1990). *The new literacy: Redefining reading and writing in the schools.* New York: Routledge.

Winterson, J. (1996). *Art objects: Essays on ecstasy and effrontery.* London: Vintage.